# ARE YOU LIVING OR JUST EXISTING?

**PLUGGED IN...**

**WHAT FUTURE DO YOU SEE?**

## Tony Sayers

## Table of Contents

Dedication ..................................................................... 2
About the Author ........................................................ 2
Introduction ................................................................. 2
1. Strange Times ........................................................ 2
2. Rampant Apathy .................................................... 2
3. The Constant Divide and DiSempowerment ....... 2
4. Just Following Orders sir ..................................... 2
5. The Big Disconnect .............................................. 2
6. Caging the Mind ................................................... 2
7. Groomed for Servitude ........................................ 2
8. The Commodity that is Nature ........................... 2
9. The Disease of Convenience .............................. 2
10. The Hidden Hands ............................................. 2
11. The Confusion Of The Sexes ........................... 2
12. What's your poison? .......................................... 2
13. Chasing Pieces of Paper .................................. 2
14. Truth Mixed With Lies ....................................... 2
15. Solutions ............................................................. 2
Self-Publishing Your Book ....................................... 2
Are you Living or Just Existing? ............................. 1

# ARE YOU LIVING OR JUST EXISTING?

Are You Living Or Just Existing?

– By Tony Sayers

Published 2018 by Sazmick Books
www.sazmickbooks.com
info@sazmickbooks.com
© Copyright 2018 Tony Sayers. All rights reserved.

No part of this book may be reproduced, stored in a retrieval system, or transmitted by any means without the written permission of the author. Please note: The views in this book are not necessarily those of the publisher.

British Library Cataloguing-in Publication Data.
A catalogue record for this book is available from the British Library.

ISBN: 978-1-912400-0-6-5
Printed and bound in the UK using sustainable resources

# *ARE YOU LIVING OR JUST EXISTING?*

Tony Sayers

# Dedication

A big thanks to my mum, dad, and the rest of my family for always supporting me even if you dont always agree with me, and adapting to me changing over the years! I love you.

Thanks also to my best friend George who always has my back, Tony Hurst at www.organicwebdesign.eu for the artwork, and to Sazmick books for your support and help throughout.

# About the Author

Tony Sayers is a passionate activist, vlogger, writer, and public speaker who in 2013 started to become aware of the deeper goings on within this World and the hidden hands that control it. Since having these realisations he has been relentless in his work to expose the levels of corruption in society in an attempt to help others open their eyes. He is driven by doing what he can in his own way to help future generations enjoy a better World. His work has been mainly focused on human psychology, mind control, and spiritual laws. He is now progressing into technological, metaphysical manipulations, and energy healing work.

Born in Southend on Sea, Essex, UK, Tony enjoyed a good childhood, although he found school quite challenging with other students and somewhat boring. His questioning of what is normal had subconsciously already began. From school Tony went travelling when he was 21 which was a huge learning curve where he felt he got a real education observing how other cultures lived, and the vast differences between the developed and non developed World. He also travelled to Nepal and researched Buddhism, which at the time was to sew a spiritual seed in him that was to germinate later in life.

After this period he went on to work in many 'normal' jobs in the Banking and Estate Agency Worlds, but never truly feeling fulfilled, and feeling as if he was 'just going through the motions' of life. It was in this period where he was so down beat in the rigourous daily grind he started to ask the big questions in life which ultimately led him to these greater understandings about himself and the World, the learning is still going on today.

Sometimes controversial, Tony is raw in how he expresses himself and his truth but is always coming from a place of care and desire for positive change. Tony has appeared on radio shows, and spoke publicly which can be found on Youtube. He has his own website which is www.transcendingtimes.org where all his work can be found.

# Introduction

So are you living or just existing? A powerful question I had to ask myself around 5 years ago. That one sentence triggered a multitude of feelings inside me and an array of thoughts and questions, many of which I didn't necessarily like the answers to. With that question other questions splintered off in my mind. Who runs the World? Why do I feel like Im on a treadmill day after day? Deep introspection followed, the answer was that I was existing and I had been for many years. Stagnating yet at the same time, an inner knowing just driving me on to find the answers. I wanted to break free of whatever cocoon I had been in all my life, I wanted my life to have meaning, a purpose, a mission even, and I intuitively felt that we all have that. The big question for me was that I hadn't even discovered mine, I was in my mid thirties and life was passing me by, I was somewhat 'successful' in my career but I never made it too far up the corporate ladder because looking back now, I understood that it was bullshit. Shmoozing and brown nosing my way up the ladder was never my style, I preferred to get results, yet even when they came because I wasn't patting the right backs and speaking up about things I shouldn't, I never made it too far up.

It was the first time in my life that I had really and truly questioned my own existence, or maybe I had but I just wasn't being honest with myself. I think we can tend to lie to ourselves the most about a whole host of things. So at the time of questioning I decided I was going to be brutally honest with myself to get some real truth and understanding. So it was an interesting time for me because no sooner had I started to ask these questions I would stumble across information, researchers, documentaries, and books that really started to paint an honest picture about the World around me. What I was to discover was the World I thought to be real along with sitations and events, when I studied and delved deeper were in fact a lot different. This then arose other questions and so on it went, and in many ways it is still going on today. The amazing thing was that after I shed the layers of not only myself and what I had been taught I actually found myself, and from that point although it hasn't been easy, especially as other people see you change so much, it has been worth it. Mainly because I am no longer lying to myself, and I see things with a rawness I hadn't done previously.

The title of the book can be quite over arching, I mean many people will read that and think well yes I am living, they may have a great job doing what they love, family, a good social network etc. But my point is even from that perspective are they living from, and are their beliefs about themselves, coming from a position of raw truth and honesty? Because for me that is the underlying message that this question poses. When I mean honest I mean brutally honest. I strongly feel unless we are brutally honest with ourselves first then how can we say we are being authentic and TRULY 'living'? So its a multifaceted question, yes you can be happy, fulfilled etc but is there true authenticy there?

Now you could be in the other camp, the camp that I was in "just existing' which in that case the book will hopefully be a real eye opener. Either way whatever camp you're in there is no right or wrong here, we are all on different parts of the road we call life. But whichever camp I hope that this book will raise an eyebrow or two and maybe just enable you to question your own reality.

I must also point out that I am not trying to make friends or create followers with this book, I didnt write this to get good reviews or anything like that. Some of the information might be challenging, its supposed to be. It is raw, unapologetic, and it is from my heart because ultimately I have written this book to encourage people to become a better version of themselves, and thus in my own small way, help to make the World a better place. I am also not saying Im perfect myself or that I have it all figured out, I am like everyone else, a work in progress. But I know one thing I am unrecognisable from 5 years ago, and I am thankfully now living. Truly.

So this book really contains much of what I have been learning about and trying to understand over the past few years, I guess what I have attempted to do is package it up into something palatable, and all I ask from you the reader is to open your mind.

# Strange Times

Such amazingly interesting times we live in right now. On the one hand we have a system in place here on this planet that is throwing the kitchen sink at humanity. Rumors of wars, financial collapse, killer viruses, and so called 'terrorist attacks' taking place around the World almost on a weekly basis from Bangkok, to Paris, from London to Orlando. On the other hand you have a population of people who are just starting to lift their heads up from the TV screens what with all the soap operas and sports programs to question the total, undeniable insanity taking place all around them right now. Quite clearly something is very wrong with the World, and for the first time in a very long time humanity is starting to stir.

As I write this book I am doing so the day after the 15th anniversary of September 11th 2001 attacks, an event which undoubtedly changed and reshaped the future of our Planet forever. Refreshingly, now more than ever, people are asking serious questions about the official version of events. I am not going to go into a full breakdown of what I believed happened that day as it would take another book to write in and of itself. What I will say though is that quite frankly a child could debunk the mainstream rhetoric. Just the fact that they couldn't find the black box from the aircraft (the only time in the history of airline crashes) yet they found the 'terrorists' passport within all that rubble, and yet jet fuel which apparently (so we're told) can melt steel beams! That's without building 7 just collapsing freefalling of its own accord without a plane even hitting it, and the BBC reporting it doing so 20 minutes before it actually fell! You can come to your own conclusions on that, my aim is to solely get you, the reader, to think critically, independently, and draw your own conclusions.

What I write in this book is a combination of my own years of dedicated research on a number of topics, and also my own ideas, concepts, and theories I have come up with myself about the human situation aswell as harnassing information from other researchers along the way. I will say now to always do your own research; this can be used as a guide to draw on your own conclusions. There are, of course, objective truths to be discovered, but these have to be discovered by you. Hopefully this book will be part of your journey to a more fuller rounded understanding of this crazy World we live in, and WHY it is the way it is. One thing that will be required is an open mind, they say the mind is like a parachute, and only works when it is open. Some of the information may be uncomfortable, abrasive, or make you feel uncomfortable at times. Yet to get a deep understanding of our situation we have to face our collective shadows in order to transcend them and turn them into something positive like true alchemists. The truth is we have been ignoring things for far too long and look where it has got us? We are facing a crucial time in our history, yet at the same time it is an absolute fascinating time to be alive. We are on the cusp of change, but to make that change long lasting and positive for generations to come we have to look at what has held us back from being the powerful, creative beings that we have always been but have just forgotten!

This journey the way I see it has to be taken from an apophatic inquiry viewpoint, which is that by looking within the negatives, the solutions can be found. Most of the solutions lie in ridding old belief systems and bad habits that have been with us for hundreds, if not thousands of years. Ultimately a huge proportion of what we are up against is all a mind game, and to even think independently in a World where everybody thinks the same is a huge achievement. To regain our minds from those that wish to control us (and there are people that wish to control us!) is half the battle. Ultimately this is what I aim to achieve in this book, to get the mind working again. Questioning, probing, nudging, and in some cases just attempting to smash apart old dogmas and so called traditions which we follow blindly. The rabbit hole goes a lot deeper than just this book, into the realms of the spiritual, technological, and metaphysical so what I am hoping is to engage the reader into the surface level as to what is considered 'normal' whilst touching on some of these other aspects.

So the first question to ask ourselves is why don't people think anymore? I mean they think, but I'm talking REALLY think? Like asking the BIG questions in life such as why am I here? What is my purpose in life? Why do the few have so much and everyone else is left to fight over the bread crumbs? Is this all there is here on Earth? Is there a God? For me the general population does not care enough to ask themselves these game changing questions. Quite frankly they're lazy. They're quite happy to let the government do the thinking for them, and it will gratefully accept that role! People just seem to want an easy life, they're quite happy with their Eastenders and X Factor at the weekend. It's too much effort to actually ponder on their own existence, or question why we live in a constant state of perpetual war. No leave that to someone else, one of those 'do-gooders'. What people don't seem to understand is that each individual has a moral responsibility to help create a better World to leave for future generations, the problem is people don't want to face up to that responsibility which is why the World is as it is. As long as people have football and beer then they're not interested. Well we are now seeing the direct consequences of those inactions and lack of care.

Now the other reason that people don't ask the groundbreaking questions is that society has been set up (by design) to keep people in survival mode. Chasing pieces of paper called money around until the day they die, attempting to put food on the table, or pay the rent. Most people earning just enough to keep their heads above water, exhausted they get to the end of the working week and the last thing they want to do is question the fact that they are the only species on the Planet that has to PAY for its own existence! Think about it, the fact that we have to pay for our basic needs as a human being namely food, water, and shelter is absolutely ludicrous! Even in China now people are buying bottles of air! Yet nobody questions the insanity of it all? They're on that treadmill we call 'life' pounding away constantly. They don't call it 'earning a living' for nothing. To EARN for the right to live? Madness. This is called 'scarcity mind control', set up by the rich 1% who herd humanity like sheep to do all the jobs they don't want to do and pay all the taxes. They have to keep us in a mindset of lack, when in actual fact we live in a World of potential abundance. Whilst we are in this mindset worrying about bills, food, and rent, we are living in fear, and when we are in a constant state of fear we can be controlled and manipulated easily because we become more reliant on the make believe 'Gods' called government. When we rely on them we give them more power and become further enslaved.

The main issue is that many folk are satisfied with this as their lot in life, or even if they're not, they don't want to rock the boat. They just want to stay in their comfort zones and in most cases quite happy to be slaves to the system. Anything for an easy life as long as I'm 'alright Jack' then that's all that matters. It's truly very sad. This is all well and good for those that want to remain in bondage until their dying days, but what about the rest of us who want to evolve and progress to something greater, those of us who understand what TRUE freedom represents? Is this as good as it gets? With all the amazing potential of human creativity are we happy to create this prison cell for ourselves? Well I for one am not. So clearly a massive part of the solution is to firstly start giving a shit! If not for you but for your children and your grandchildren. Its surely time that each and everyone of us starts facing up to our responsibility that we are ALL keepers of this

Planet, and that it is imperative that we contribute to making sure it becomes a more free, peaceful, and loving place. It's not getting any better, this is not going away, and it's time to face up to what we have allowed to be created. So it's vital then that we ask ourselves individually what am I doing to upkeep my side of the bargain?

# Rampant Apathy

As we delve into the whys of how things are and looking at other reasons why people choose not to act or even care we firstly have to tackle this deeply problematic mindset of 'well its always been this way'. I literally cringe when I hear this being said, it's pathetically weak, and just downright lazy. Frankly it's embarrassing. The very REASON things are like they are is because people think in this manner. Their imagination has been so shot to pieces that they cannot even possibly envisage a World free from suffering. Again did we just come here to exist? To learn nothing? To grow? It's literally an acceptance of the very chains around your ankles, and furthermore plays into the hands of people who want more power over you. If you already accept that nothing can change, and that it has always been like this then we may as well all just pack our bags and go home now. Individually what does that say about a person? They are defeated; there is no self-confidence, and certainly no self-love. There cannot be because if you truly loved yourself you wouldn't allow yourself to be manipulated in such a manner. We have to regain our confidence and remember who and what we are. We are powerful, creative beings with so much unlocked potential if only we would see that in ourselves. Yet we hold each other back all the time. People say that they want to be confident, but the truth is society will attempt to put down or hold back anyone who rediscovers that confidence within themselves. They will be accused of being arrogant or egotistical. If we are being honest with ourselves, society in general doesn't seem to like people who flourish, so it begs the question do we even want to flourish as a society at all?

To me it seems we have been at rock bottom for so long the human race doesn't even know how to even start lifting itself backing up again. We have to start encouraging each other for doing the positive things, encouraging each other's innate creative talents, and find the courage and desire within to reach for the stars and get out of that 'little me' mindset. This has to be done collectively not only on an individual level too. Will we become a failed race of nobodies who just exist so others can feed and parasite from our hard labor and energy? Or do we take back the wheel of the car and blossom into the wonderful species I know deep down we can be? It can be done; we see it in Nature, the caterpillar's metamorphosis into a butterfly so to speak. We can do it, we just need to start believing in ourselves again, and that can only come when we understand ourselves at a deep level, which can only ultimately come from a thirst for knowledge. A thirst to WANT to know the truth about not only ourselves, but the World around us, and to look at the shadow side and face it head on.

This is 'learned helplessness' we have developed over hundreds if not thousands of years, and the worst thing is that there are others that are THRIVING from this mental disease, and have been for centuries. Whilst we remain lackluster and needy, those in governments and higher are only too happy to play babysitter. The problem is however, that they are literally the babysitters from hell! Now I will be talking a lot about society and the 'hive mind' in this book. I have a general rule of thumb these days that if a society thinks a certain way then I immediately run 100 miles per hour in the other direction! Culture is a cult in and of itself, break down the word and its telling you exactly that. CULT-ure, need I say more? You only have to look at how as a society we not only accept War, but we actually feel it necessary, and worse still glorify it! The issue becomes worse in that anyone who thinks outside of the box, or out of line with societal 'norms' is automatically considered as crazy, a nutjob, or a conspiracy theorist. So we actually police each other to think in set ways laid out by certain political correctness boundaries. If a person expresses their own individuality, thoughts, and ideas, then they are more often than not, put down by the rest of the cult for stepping out of line. This is a viscous circle because humans need connection, and feel comfortable within a group setting, so the vast majority keep quiet and shut up for the fear of ridicule and isolation from the rest of the sheep in the pen. Fear from being shunned out and segregated from the herd makes people end up living their whole existence living out other peoples versions of how they should think, act, speak, and ultimately live, which 99.9% of the time is only in alignment with their own slavery. Why are people so obsessed with being liked by everyone else? First of all it's boring! We are all born unique individuals with different qualities, talents, and ideas. What is the obsession with fitting in? Surely being the ONLY one of us ever in existence we should be expressing ourselves and our individuality? Be bold, express yourself, make your life a work of art, don't hold back, and most of all be you. The World needs you to express yourself, that is WHY you were born, so what are you waiting for? Approval from people that half the time don't even like themselves?

The fear of what other people think of us is the greatest prison we can ever live in. It holds us back in life, living a false and inauthentic life. It means that our lives have been a lie in effect because we just wanted to be another robot to 'fit in'. When you express the TRUE version of yourself life changes. You feel an inner peace which is coming from being in alignment with your soul, and being true to yourself. You move out of the inauthentic and into the authentic life. I know I've been there. For years I tried to fit in, never upset the apple cart. It was boring. I literally felt a life half lived. My life started when I started to question the programming, and I'm infinitely grateful that I did. So clearly a key solution is to lay off the policing of each other, lets encourage growth, encourage free thinking, and encourage our uniqueness and individuality. Until the vast majority of us start doing the inner work needed to lose the fear of what others think of us then we will continue to hold ourselves back. I'm not just talking about not caring what strangers think, I'm talking about not caring what our friends, teachers, siblings, parents, spouse, or the government thinks! Yes respect, sure. But being dictated by others either directly or indirectly on how you choose to express yourself is a mental cage. It is fact that one of the biggest reasons people are scared to express their uniqueness is for fear of what those closest to them will think or say. Well it's not their life it's yours. Always walk your own path. No opinion of some guru, teacher, or even parent is higher than your own. Be you, be amazing, and by default you will be helping the World immensely. Let's regain our confidence and move out of this defeatist mindset once and for all, and that horrible 'little me syndrome' which is basically the idea that you have no power to do or change anything in the World. You CAN.

We are ALL ripples in the pond, and by stepping up you also inspire others to do the same. Ghandi once famously said 'Be the change you wish to see in the World' Never has a truer word been spoken, He also came out with another great quote when he said 'my life is my message to the World' what is your message going to be? When you're on your death bed what mark did you leave on the World? Or were you just another number in the system? Somebody that never questioned anything, lived in fear, or just wanted to be like by everyone so you could be safe in your comfort zone? These are harsh questions but I feel absolutely necessary for anyone who wants to grow and help make this World a better place. I haven't always asked them myself, but I'm dam sure I'm glad that I eventually did in the end, because in asking those big game changing questions in life, you will find your purpose I guarantee that much, and ultimately your very reason for living.

One of the most pressing issues we face and one of which more and more researchers are talking about is humanities absolute blind belief in authority. The simple fact is that we live in a World where some are classed as 'rulers' and others 'slaves'. Oh don't get me wrong they do well to dress it up to make it look like we're not slaves with all the fancy gadgets we have nowadays, oh and thats not forgetting the 22 out 365 days a year 'holiday' that we are allowed, thanks for that! The harsh truth is let's face it, that if you want any kind of decent living standard in the so called 'developed world' you will generally have to work a minimum of a 50/60 hour a week if not more. This goes on week after week, month after month, and year after year, and if you are lucky enough to live in the UK they now want you to do this until the age of 70! Doesn't sound very 'free' to me. Again ll use the UK as an example, at last count it works out that the UK tax payer pays over 60% of their earnings on over 300 income taxes! These taxes range from anything to car tax, council tax, all the way down to pastry taxes where now you cannot even buy a pie without being taxed on it. Yet nobody questions it? Worse over you have bankers, politicians, large corporations (who make billions from the UK tax payers) and the monarchy, all paying either nothing or as close to nothing as possible, or its all tied up in off shore accounts in tax havens such as Monaco or Dubai. There is a word for this and that word is slavery which comes in many different forms other than the stereotypical ball and chain around the ankle. We have been sold down the river a long time ago folks. Grinding our knuckles until we drop dead for parasites that call themselves our 'leaders' isn't it about time we wake up to this scam? Add to the fact that most of our taxes go on weapons and bombs that blow up innocent women and children and destroy their homes. We are continuously feeding the war machine, nobody wants war yet we're paying for it? Companies such as Lockheed Martin, Boeing, and Halliburton turning up at events across the globe to promote the new killing machines they have invented. It's a sick World, but how have we allowed this to happen?

It's all deeply rooted in the mental psyche of humanity. We are like babies who want babysitters to wipe our backsides because we have not grown up as a species. Sadly we look up to them, we rely on them, we depend on them for our so called 'safety' yet we are not safe. Look around you, continuous war, austerity, poverty, homelessness, hunger, and division. What is there to respect? Continuously lying to us, why is it that whoever we vote for we always have war? We are the ones having to grind away day after day whilst they sit in their ivory towers barking out orders and rules, yet they don't even play the game themselves! As I write this I can feel the anger and frustration rage inside of me that we are so weak willed and weak minded to have allowed this to go on. It all boils down ultimately to the mental disease that is the belief in authority and government that another person or group of people have the right to tell you what to do and how to live. We are being used slaves, yet at our core nothing could be further from that. When you are born on this Planet, you are born by the very grace of the Universe a SOVEREIGN being, never were you meant to be 'ruled over' or ordered around by anyone. We must stop thinking and acting like slaves, and start shaking those chains that have held our minds in bondage for eons, release yourself from your mental cage and realize who and what you REALLY are.The only law you ever have to adhere to is Universal Natural Law, which is simply 'cause no harm or loss to other beings' EVERYTHING else is man made and exists nowhere in Nature. Be your own leader always.

But yet we keep running back to these puppets. Even those who have become aware in recent years of the fact that we are being badly duped and misled still want to see them as the solution?? We still want to give our power away to yet more wolves in sheep clothing, politicians who, on the face of it at least, appear nice and friendly and have our best interests at heart and then of course at the final hour change into the parasite they REALLY are once they have everyone's support. It happens every single time it's getting boring now. When has a politician TRULY ever served the people? It is my opinion that we are being ushered by something greater to evolve right now. I believe we are here to learn self-responsibility, self-ownership, self sovereignty, and basically to start standing on our own two feet, it's time to give up the dummies and nappies. The way I see it is that you can break the issue down into three separate components. Firstly it's a lack of confidence and belief in ourselves to not only just function, but to thrive in a World without government. I've seen people's faces when you mention it, pure terror and fear written all over their faces! God forbid the nanny state won't be there to spoon feed them.

We have to start developing the courage to take our first baby steps, to push the boundaries, and to once and for all, step up to the plate in terms of what our potential is.Secondly it boils down to a massive lack of imagination on most people's part. As inherently the creative beings that we all are, if we cannot even imagine a World without maniac rulers then it certainly won't ever manifest in the real World. I mean how chaotic could the World be without lying, war mongering, tax evaders?! Yet people think there would be chaos when that is what we already have! NEWSFLASH this Planet right now is in total chaos, and who do we have 'leading' and pulling the strings? GOVERNMENT. This is what a World with authority looks like. So again courage and imagination is needed, indeed any great positive change is nearly always preceded with chaos even in our own individual lives. Think about a time where things got completely out of hand for you, more often than not when everything has settled down and you look back, it was normally for the best right? Well same applies here. Certainly in my own life a new positive beginning has almost always started with a certain amount of disruption and pain beforehand. We as a collective need to do the same thing face things head on and hit it like a train until we come out to the other side. Personally I would much rather run the risk of some chaos in the World if it meant future generations would thrive. It will be worth it, and actually there isn't really a choice in the matter.

The third aspect of this Religious worship of the State and government is 'Stockholm Syndrome' which for those that haven't heard of it, is based around a bank siege in Stockholm, Sweden that happened 44 years ago where there were a number of hostages taken who after 6 days being held as captive started to develop some kind of sympathy and positive relationship for their captors. They actually defended their actions, almost like a kind of worship mentality. Similar to the master/slave dynamic we have going on here on Earth. This is exactly what is taking place around us.

Take the Queen of England as a prime example, here is a women who sits on literally billions of pounds, she wears a golden hat and sits on a golden chair. Yet look at the people that she is supposed to 'serve' in the UK. Austerity is rife, people living out of food banks, and homelessness at an all time high. Yet what is she doing to help her people? She doesn't even pay any taxes! Yet sit down and watch one of her birthday or jubilee events and you will see a literal vomit fest of peasants cheering for their master. Millions of people worshipping her like flag waving lunatics. Even singing a song about her that even has the classic slave tag line 'long to reign over us'! This woman could wipe out World poverty with the stroke of a pen on a blank chequebook! So why doesn't she then? Because she couldn't give a flying f*** that's why! We are making absolute fools of ourselves, kissing the feet of the very people that are whipping our backsides day in and day out. Enough of this mental insanity wake up and smell the coffee. These people are LAUGHING at us, using our hard labor to their own advantage, and getting US to fight their Wars! The mockery is also right in our faces too, what does that tie around your neck remind you of when you leave to go to work each morning? Could it be a NOOSE around your neck? Our very uniforms are symbolic of slavery. Stop the worship, stop the praise, and stop singing songs about people that USE your entire body, mind, and souls to further their own agendas.

# THE CONSTANT DIVIDE AND DISEMPOWERMENT

Of course what they have done for centuries now is divide and pit the population continuously against each other, this is because whilst we are at odds with each other we will not pay any attention to the REAL reason that the Planet is in constant turmoil. Have you ever stopped to notice how they constantly talk about our differences and not our similarities? They never talk about the fact that fundamentally we are, at our core, just one big human family. We may have many different belief systems, Religions and cultures, but ultimately we all bleed the same blood. No it's always black versus white, rich versus poor, gay versus straight, Christians against Muslims, and men versus women. This is done relentlessly, day after day using the very media that they own and control, all because that whilst we fight amongst each other they can get away with literal murder. Even Nations and borders, who even invented those? These imaginary lines in the sand do not exist anywhere in Nature, when the World was created, and we can debate how it was at another time, whether or not that was due to a 'big bang' or some creative force, there were never any Countries in the beginning? Why do we need all this documentation to cross from one piece of land to another? We are human beings and by the grace of the Universe we are allowed to roam freely anywhere we like on the Planet. For a man in a suit to tell me I cannot go here or there is absolutely absurd. Yet again though it has simply been accepted as 'normal'. It really is the ultimate division tactic, which ties in with the mental disease of patriotism, which I will touch on later. England versus Germany, USA versus Russia, Spain versus France etc. Divide, divide, and divide. We are ALL brothers and sisters here on Earth, the difference we have in our cultures should be celebrated as part of our uniqueness not used as a tool to pit us against each other. We have to start finding some kind of unity and all come together against the common enemy, we ALL face the same manipulation wherever we are in the World, some feel it more than others granted, but still let's stop bickering and allowing ourselves to be so divided. We need to come together like never before, our very future as a species relies on us doing so.

As I write this book there is a huge focus on Muslims and Islam around the World, the mainstream media is ramping this up like never before and people in their droves are falling for it, hook, line, and sinker. Its absolute garbage being propagated, things like Sharia Law is going to be imposed on people the World over, or that folk are somehow going to be FORCED to eat Halal meat. Absolutely ridiculous stories to ramp up fear, division, and hate. The gusto people seem to buy into it all is very worrying, it's almost like people WANT to hate. People like this are just projecting an aspect of their inner self. The truth is that they WANT to hate on something because ultimately at some level they hate themselves. Don't fall for it because by doing so you are playing the game they want you to play, which then also makes YOU part of the problem. If you don't like sharing the Planet with other cultures then go and find another Planet because this one is based on diversity, free will, and is all part of the human experience. I'm not saying that the faith of Islam is not without its problems, all Religions are. But there are bad Christians, bad Jews, and bad Catholics too, it's just you don't hear about those ones because the agenda is to ramp up as much hate as possible against Islam, which is playing the fall guy in the grander scheme of things.

Whilst on the subject of division it seems apt at this point to talk about Religion. I'm not going to go into the ins and outs of each one, for me I like to keep things simple. Religion ALL of them were created by the ruling class as just another way to 'divide and rule' over humanity. The fact is that even the most basic of common sense tells me that they are absolutely crazy, I mean for example here we have supposedly an 'all loving God' who will send you to 'Hell' or 'Hellfire' just for not believing in him?? I mean surely that would be a major red flag right? I would have imagined that the creator of everything wouldn't be so insecure as to need everyone to worship him! You would have thought he would come from a place of unconditional love and free will? A God that expects folk to get up at 4am EVERY day to disturb their sleep, just to start worshiping him! Crazy. Of course this is all perfect for a force which seeks to control the population. I mean here we have a species arguing and fighting over whose God is best! The concerning issue is that in my dealings with Religious folk they are willing to accept that we have been lied to about almost EVERTHING else health, politics, history etc EXCEPT their Religion! Let's face it there will never be any true unity amongst the population whilst Religion is hanging around, it needs to go far far away if we are ever to have peace on Earth. Again without going into too many details as I am trying to cover as many concepts and ideas as possible in this book, there are some truths thrown into Religions, there has to be to get people hooked, they have to get people interested in the first place. Religions at their core, underneath all the bullshit speak in allegories, messages or fairytales that are telling us things about human consciousness itself in a covert way. They are actually truly fascinating when you research into their TRUE meanings. They were never supposed to have been taken literally, and the fact that they have is truly quite embarrassing for humanity as a species.

It's the same with the whole 'New Age' pseudo spiritual movement at the moment. Truth mixed with a whole load of lies.

Personally I consider myself a spiritual man but I see the pitfalls and diversion techniques that keep people away from their true power. Looking outside of themselves for a savior constantly whether it is angelic beings, aliens, or the Galactic Federation of Light! For me as well as division the biggest pitfall with Religion is people giving their personal power away. It's the ultimate weakness mankind has in my opinion. Always looking for someone or something to come and save themselves, there is always some corrupt politician or God ready to come and solve all our problems. It's pretty clear to me that after hundreds and thousands of years of both voting and praying, it's really not working out for us too well is it? Any loving God would have answered our prayers to stop War and famine millennia ago! The 'right' politician would have been also voted in by now if government truly did represent any kind of democracy. The truth is, and this is what they dont want you to realise, YOU are your OWN savior, humanity is our own savior. We are here to learn self-responsibility as I have already said. WE have to sort this mess out ourselves and it is not going to be easy. Nobody is coming down from sitting on their cloud, there is no 'knight in shining armor,' and there is certainly not another puppet politician coming to begin the road to peace. You cannot be TRULY conscious if you are looking for anyone outside of yourself to save or lead you. Be your own God, hero, leader, and savior. Ultimately this is what this is all about, evolving to lead ourselves?

Of course it goes without saying that those in control want to keep it this way, whilst 7 billion people are consistently giving their power away to different 'leaders' they will never realize their own personal empowerment and TRUE sovereignty. A powerful population with people that have woken up to their own magnificence is much harder to bully around! You personally have a choice, keep thinking and acting like a needy slave handing over your dwindling rights and freedoms daily, or wake up to your potential and realise what you REALLY are and become part of a new conscious, caring, and courageous group of people ready to catapult this World into a new existence. The choice is truly yours. Sovereign or slave?The main objective of the ruling class as mentioned previously is getting folk to look outside of themselves, and the State is only too happy to step in and play the role of God in people's minds, so much so that the Stockholm syndrome mentality has led to this whole disease of the mind called 'patriotism' whereby people identify so much with a piece of land that they just so happened to be born on, that there are even some that would be willing to give their lives, or take the lives of others because they feel such a strong affinity to this particular piece of land. If however you don't agree with the State or question the absurdity of it all you are then somehow considered some kind of 'traitor'. Every law and rule has to be accepted without question because we are told that its 'good for the Country'. Rights and freedoms being eroded almost by the hour because the economy, national security, or whatever the official line may be demands it. Then you have the folk that will actually go and start violence at sporting events like football, waving their flags in the worship of their own special prison cells, and they cannot even see the bars!

Let's be honest about this, the mental disease that is patriotism allows the State to get away with whatever it wants including theft, violence, and murder, and yet millions of flag waving morons have no idea of any depth to what it is they are actually supporting. It gives the State free reign. The people within that particular prison cell that we call a 'Country' are constantly being bombarded by the government mouthpiece media outlets telling people how "great' their piece of land is, and how 'proud' they should all be. Its classic mind manipulation and when it is repeated constantly from childhood people grow up embodying it completely. Again its classic 'divide and rule' pitting nations off against each other, getting people to dislike each other because they live within another imaginary border. In many cases even to hate their neighboring prison cell. It's all tribe mentality, and it's like that by design. Patriotism excuses any kind of bad behavior from the State, and as I mentioned, particularly when it comes to war where we have this gut wrenchingly sick continuous propaganda to 'support the troops' or 'support our boys' etc. Yet nobody questions what they are doing or why?? It's just blind faith, and people, INNOCENT people are DYING as a result of this blind belief and support of government! Because it's not 'loyal' to question anything the State does is it? No let's just bomb a Country, steal its oil and resources, you peasants just shut up and wave your flags! It's also the sheer amount of hate patriotism generates with outlandish claims that certain people 'shouldn't be allowed in' because it's 'our Country' no it's just a piece of land that your parents happened to have sex on! It's like these people OWN this land.

The land belongs to Nature, the Planet; it doesn't belong to one person or a group of people! The hypocrisy of it all is sickening, where if you take the UK right now many will moan that immigrants coming into the Country should 'speak our language' yet here we have nearly 1 million British expats living in Spain, that couldn't even order a taxi in Spanish and expect all the restaurants to serve an English fry up and Carlsberg lager! Get over yourselves! It's the same with the whole 'we need to look after our own first' right ok then when was the last time YOU personally went out and fed the homeless who are being arrested and fined just for being homeless?! Silence. Because they don't. Hypocrites as I say, their minds have been manipulated as they follow whatever opinions the 'news' tells them to. Brainwashed totally. If you're going to call out immigrants, and what is expected, at least be consistent across all levels.

If people actually stopped for one second and thought about what it actually is that they are getting behind here and what it represents. The hysteria is ramped up to cosmic levels when we have these now celebrity figureheads wheeled out to the masses, whether that be a president, prime minister, or a member of the Royal family. If it's a birthday, jubilee, or anniversary maximum patriotism is required by the herds, what this does is generate even more loyalty to our masters, the kids get involved, and they grow up to be slave worshippers too, cheering for their own particular cage, and thus the cycle continues.

The hive mind comes into this again, because most people are loyal to the state and if anyone comes along and dares to critisise the actions of their Country they are met with great resistance. Is it any surprise when you consider that from a very early age in school we are force fed how 'great our nation' is. Yet we never get told the full story, the other side of the coin, or know about the horrific consequences of our actions? Were you ever taught about the murder of millions of aborigines, or Native Americans from the white man? How we stole their land, food, and raped their women? What about the weapons of mass destruction that were never found in Iraq when we went and killed one million Iraqis? Do you think that will be taught in the history lessons? No let's just glorify and support EVERYTHING without question. Rule Britannia the nation with so much blood on its hands it is nearly drowning! The sad thing is that children take these concepts into adult life and guess who benefits again? You guessed it, the prison wardens, or better known as government or authority. Get them to love and worship their own prison cells, waving silly little flags and they certainly won't question that they are in fact prison cells. It's the way these flags are used when it comes to the military, it's quite sickening draping the flag over young mens coffins that are sent to murder themselves, all for what? Is it REALLY to fight so called 'terrorists'? The same terrorists in Al Quaeda, ISIS, and the Mujahedeen that were ALL trained and funded by western governments? Why does it always seem to be some oil and resource rich nation in the Middle East that always needs a dose of our 'freedom'? Iraq, Libya, and now more recently Syria. There is always some 'boogieman' that is out to get us all, Saddam Hussein, Gaddafi, Bin Laden, and now Assad. Let just forget about the millions that Bush, Regan, Obama, Blair, and Cameron maimed and killed? I would suggest many millions more than those so called 'dictators'.They send young men out to these places to do the dirty work for them, and if they don't come back dead then they either suicide, or are left homeless with no help or support by the very people who sent them?! What is it all about, and what the Hell are we doing here??

# Just Following Orders sir

I really don't have sympathy for military personnel. Although they are not making the actual decisions to go to War and to fight, fundamentally they are the ones that are pulling the triggers and dropping the bombs. It is them even more so than governments who need to start taking responsibility for their actions for causing so much chaos, and for the very reason that this World constantly exists in a state of conflict. It is no longer acceptable now in the 21st century to use the lame excuse 'just following orders'. There needs to be culpability, moral compasses need to be engaged once and for all, this is not a game. Innocent women and children get blown up, homes destroyed, limbs blown off, cancer causing chemicals like depleted uranium being dropped devastating the long term health of hundreds of thousands of people ensuring that future generations are born with defects. Brains needs to be engaged not guns! The World is tired of War now and soldiers, and we as the general public need to question HARD the reasons for these wars. Every single one of us has to take personal responsibility and speak out, and ultimately soldiers need to put their guns down. Let the politicians go to war and fight amongst themselves, let's see if they send their own to fight? Not just the William and Harry charade which is just a dog and pony show to make it look like the ruling class actually get their hands dirty in these conflicts. Let's stop even calling it War, let's call it what it really is which simply organized murder. Until the military start thinking for themselves then it's down to the public to withdraw support. We all have blood on our hands when we allow this to pass unchecked. Not in my name, whilst I am here I will not support these illegal invasions into Countries that have done us no direct harm.

Surely the whole idea of 'following orders' is an inherently diseased and backwards mindset? As a sovereign being you have free will and YOU decide what you should or shouldn't do. It is YOU that decides what is right or wrong, and ultimately it is YOU that must live with the consequences of those actions, and military personnel believe me there ARE consequences. Nobody determines what is moral or immoral other than your own conscience. Yet soldiers will insist until they are blue in the face that they are thinking for themselves, but really by definition if you are following orders then you CANNOT in any way, shape, or form be engaging your own brain and moral compass because you have passed the very decision making process over to somebody else. Enough of this disgraceful glorification of death and murder dressed up in patriotism, it's high time we finally put an end to Wars on this Godforsaken planet! Yet it's so simple to see that the only people that ever benefit from Wars are the ones that always want them in the first place! How do the soldiers benefit? Depression? PTSD? Anxiety? Plus the fact they get paid peanuts to kill too, talk about rubbing salt into the literal wounds. Certainly it goes without saying the civilians don't benefit at all. You can bet your life that the western governments and the weapons manufacturers do though, all giving each other back handers the same time as the state owned media is scaring the public into agreeing with yet more death and violence.

The solution couldn't be simpler on this one. Military put down your dam weapons! Start thinking for yourself and disobeying immoral orders, or at least before you join up make sure you have an in depth view of the World and who runs it! People will say that this is Utopia and there will always be War. This is true because there will only ever be War as long as there are people willing to fight in them. As I have said previously, the World we have allowed to be created doesn't HAVE to be this way; we can create whatever we want. Why do we accept this? Why have we allowed this decade after decade? And why do soldiers continue to fight in them despite knowing the depth of government lies? Whilst writing this book new information has come to light that the Pentagon paid half a billion dollars to a British company to make fake terrorist and propaganda videos! This was MAINSTREAM MEDIA reporting. I mean how blatantly obvious has it got to be here? That for me was a line in the sand as far as the military goes. If you're going to continue to follow orders from governments making fake videos then you really aren't interested in fighting for peoples freedoms like you say you are, How can ones conscience allow them to fight under these circumstances?

Sadly I can only conclude that the military revel in the 'hero' status that is bestowed upon them by the brainwashed, flag waving public. They parade around with their medals which look like (by design as a form of mockery) dog tags, given to them by the controllers as a 'thank you very much for being a good pet and doing our dirty work for us'. Chests are pumped out and the glory worship starts, it's sickening, vile in fact.Yet I will say this we DO need the military at this time in history, we need them to join us in the battle for TRUE freedom, to join the good fight. Against those who use and mock them, discard them, and ultimately get them to enslave others in our human family. If there are any military folk reading this, or indeed anyone else in occupations that support this immoral system based in fear and violence. Police, bailiffs etc. then I urge you to think about what I am saying here. Is a pay cheque worth your very soul as a human being? Do you want this on your conscience when you are lying on your death bed? That in actual fact it was YOU that were part of the problem in this World? That you were fighting, protecting, and serving people who couldn't give a f*** about you or your family? I know I wouldn't want that on my conscience, I couldn't even bare being an Estate Agent in the end! It's not too late either; if you have served or are currently serving you can turn things around. Come back to your TRUE family, your human family. We are waiting for you, and we need you now more than ever. And to the droves of people flag waving, what does that flag you wave REALLY stand for? Think and question, then question again.

Of course a big part of the issue here is that the military are generally segregated from the rest of society, this is also by design as a siege mentality needs to be created, that brotherhood, us against them. To expose the ranks to the general public is extremely risky because not everyone agrees with War. They can't have others putting doubts in the minds of our young 'heroes' now can they? Also they are recruited at such a young age it's insane! Join the Cadets, great just out of school where you can learn how to die in a pointless and unnecessary conflict. Recruitment starts disgustingly early, how can a 15 or 16 year old boy who has not even started adult life decide that they want to take part in War? It's a form of child abuse is what it is! And what are the parents thinking encouraging this behavior? Parents aren't just trying to discourage this, they are actively ENCOURAGING it. Just imagine a World where we send young boys off to kill and be killed. Well you don't have to, it's here and you're living in it! The areas targeted for recruitment are also some of the poorest in the Country, homing in on the desperate as accurately as their million pound missiles. Focus on areas where opportunities are limited where the people are desperate and you have another generation willing to take the bullets for you. Perfect for a sick set of warmongers to groom their next minions.

Another term I hear all the time to excuse the actions of the military is 'collateral damage'. If I had a pound for every time I have heard this phrase I would be a very rich man. That it's all just 'par for the course' or that it is just a 'natural consequence' of conflict. Well why don't you try telling that to a father who has witnessed his baby girl being blown up into pieces?? Tell him that it was just 'collateral damage'! Tell the elderly couples that have had their home blown to smithereens that it's just a 'natural consequence' these are the realities of War that we have been so desensitized to for so many years. But they don't show all that on the BBC or CNN do they? No just pictures of an odd missile being fired from distance, or a town being so called 'liberated' conveniently leave the horrors out of it. That part has to be kept as far away from the general public as possible otherwise they would lose support overnight. Thank God for the internet now where these poor victims can film the atrocities, the pain, death, and violence that is REALLY being bestowed upon them. These images can no longer be hidden, and as horrific as they are, at least give the full low down on what goes on. That is, of course, if people acknowledge it and don't bury their heads in the sand. 'Oh I don't like looking at that" I hear, REALLY? Poor you and your feelings, how do you think that Palestinian felt? The Syrian child felt? If you don't like seeing those images then get off your backside and do something about it, and stop it from happening ever again!

It seems like I am singling out the military here, and maybe I am a bit, I'm just fed up of it all. I have friends in Gaza, friends that tell me about the horrors of their reality, how kids are left homeless with no food or family to speak of. They tell me of the terrifying noise the bombs make as they are rocketing in, wondering whether or not their home will be hit, or whether they will even live a few more hours, let alone days. I have cried talking to friends in Palestine, lost contact with them thinking they were dead. These are real people like you and I please start caring about them like you would your own family. It's the stamping all over people's rights from people who blindly obey orders and are; let's face it, serving absolutely evil people. Just the fact that a police officer will arrest and throw somebody into a cage if they happen to be growing a certain plant, yet a government official, or high profile member of society who is suspected of child abuse does not even get investigated properly?? Why is it that those people higher up and with more power get wrapped up in cotton wool, yet us mere mortals are lambasted and punished if we step even slightly out of line?? How can it be right that a politician who has several properties, and has been caught red handed evading tax get away with it scott free, yet if you or I don't fill in our tax return forms on time we can be violently taken away, and thrown into a cell? If we resist this unfairness and punishment in anyway we are more than likely going to suffer a beating too! Yet people honestly think that they are free? They wouldn't know what true freedom was if it smacked them straight between the eyes. Because at some level they LOVE it this way, they are comfortable in their servitude, at some deep level within themselves they feel that they DESERVE to be treated in such a way, that they are not worthy of true freedom. A person with any amount of self-love or self-respect would resist this wholeheartedly. Only folk who self loathe would put up with being treated in such a way. Yet that is the majority of humanity, it is the harsh truth that most humans are in a mental state of self-loathing, they might not be consciously aware of it, but it is rooted deep in their subconscious minds, that is one of the main reasons people do not resist.

The Police are just tools for the government to do what they like to us. Put on a uniform and they lose their minds, they become something so disconnected from the rest of us. People that, like the military, do not think for themselves, and just act out any old orders on someone else's say so, doesn't matter how immoral that order may be. Anything goes because they have to pick up their monthly wage, ironic when you consider the police are SUPPOSED to be serving the people when they take their oath! They no longer serve the people, its really just one big extortion raquet these days. Its all about trying to catch people out, sitting and hiding on roadsides pointing speed cameras at people, or issuing petty fines, or now like I mentioned before fining and arresting homeless people for being homeless, way to go, what would we do without them! It's the police violence that has massively increased nowadays, I think back to my youth growing up in the 80s where it was common to see the 'Bobby' out on his own talking to folk, and generally they were quite approachable. Nowadays they are like Military, carrying weapons, and armor, the videos of people being tasered are absolutely horrific. I've seen women and children being stunned by these things, and then kicked and beaten. You cannot even protest or speak out against the government without them getting involved. I don't feel 'safe' when I see the Police, I feel guilty and intimidated before I have even done anything wrong.

Don't be fooled they're not protecting you, theyre protecting the system, the corporations, and the boundaries of free speech. The Police state is not on its way folks, its already here.

A huge part of the solution has to be trying to reach the minds of these people. Being blunt with them, letting them know that what they are doing is completely unacceptable, we have to start withdrawing all support for these brutal organisations the Military and the Police. Here's an idea why don't we have a 'Lets not support the troops' day?? Their very existence of supposedly protecting the people is a charade. The Military take away people's rights abroad, and the Police do it here. In the US there are far more deaths due to police brutality than so called 'terrorist attacks.' We are moving so fast into an Orwellian World it is shocking. Free speech is hanging by a literal thread, and when Orwell himself talked about 'thought Police' in his book 1984 he wasn't too far off the mark! Soon the day will come when even thinking anything negative about the State will result in a beating and imprisonment, and it will be the same mindless people that will do anything for a wage, and think that somehow 'mans law' is even relevant on this Planet, because once again its not! The law of the Universe as I have said is all that matters, don't harm others, don't steal. Everything else doesn't need to be 'upheld' because it doesn't exist! Normal human beings thinking they have the right to coerce others by brute force because they wear a silly uniform, and some figurehead in authority who signed a useless piece of paper told them it was ok to do so. WRONG you have no right to do this, all you are 'enforcing' are control mechanisms put in place that will ensure the long term enslavement of YOUR OWN children and grandchildren!

The ironic thing here is that from a Universal point of view it is actually the government cronies in organisations like the Police that are breaking the Law, they are breaking Universal Law EVERY day by taking away the rights and freedoms of others. They ARE causing harm, causing loss to others, using violence, and locking people up for the tiniest of things. YOU are the law breakers, and trust me you will have to face the consequences because you might think you are safe and comfortable and that the government protects your immoral behavior, but NOTHING escapes Universal Law and there is such a thing called Karma, and it is very real. You by behaving in this manner are accruing some very bad karma to come so just think about that next time you go to fine someone for living on the streets! Take a step back and think about what it is you are part of and what it is you are actually serving and what it stands for. Do you really want to represent that? A system that is eroding the freedoms of your fellow men, women, and children? YOU are the one ensuring that this happens, its not the government at all, its you because you are the one carrying out the PHYSICAL ACTION to bring this into manifestation. It will be YOUR children and grandchildren that have to grow up in this Police state. Please stop and think because humanity is relying on you heavily to do so. Or if you are going to bully and lock someone up, do it to those that are starting the illegal Wars, evading taxes, and abusing our children, not some guy in a flat who is peacefully smoking a plant and wants to just chill out, or some passionate activist who cares about change and wants to voice their opinion unhindered!

Just what is it with uniforms I ask? Give a man or woman a silly outfit and hat and they lose their minds?? Their ego goes through the roof, its like they put on some kind of superman outfit or something and morph into somebody completely different. Someone who is on a power trip, somebody who completely loses all sense of their humanity. It has to be something wrong that is deep rooted within their very psychological make up to want to dominate so much? Were they bullied at school? Unloved by their parents? Do they lack the confidence in themselves that when they put on this fancy dress they can be somebody entirely different? It's like an alter ego. For me again it comes down to self love, if you truly love and respect yourself, that by default will extend out to others. If you are bullying people around, throwing them in cells, and stamping all over their rights and freedoms, what does that say about that individual? It tells me that they are lacking in something. They have to be to want to do that job. It makes them feel big, powerful, and above others.

The problem is of course two fold though because as long as we have men and women willing to carry out the orders, there are BILLIONS of people willing to obey them unquestioningly. We the people are just as culpable for creating this huge open air prison through our continued aquiesence to unjust laws. There is literally ZERO resistance to any of this. Its all about comply, comply, comply. Unfortunately when we never resist anything they get worse, which is exactly what we are seeing now. When we see a man or woman in fancy dress we immediately give our power away, and we believe OURSELVES that this human being has authority over us and can tell us what to do, and order us about just because they have a silly uniform on.

I was shocked one day when I helped to organize a march in London to protest genetically modified food, and in particular the evil organization that is Monsanto (soon to be Bayer) I was given a simple bright yellow orange UV jacket to wear. I actually found it hilarious because automatically you were shown IMMEDIATE respect! I could stop the flow of traffic, redirect it, I could (if I had wanted) stop people from entering certain areas, or literally just tell people what to do. I only told people what was necessary, and redirected in line with how the event needed me to redirect but my point is I COULD have done anything! Suddenly I had all this power and nobody, not one person questioned me, they just did whatever they were all told! Because I had this special orange bib people automatically projected me as a figure of authority, a very interesting experiment to say the least!

Yet in many way if it wasn't so tragic it would be hilarious because this is how we act to people in uniform. Doing exactly what they tell us to do, when, where, and how. It is man's willingness to obey authority no matter how absurd the law or request is which is both a massive part of the problem but also a huge part of the solution at the same time. Conforming at every turn to rules made by others that have no basis in existence. A license for more or less everything these days, and fines being issued for the smallest irrelevances, of which barely any are rooted in causing harm or loss to others. They are, as I say, methods of control or coercion tactics to extract money from the public. What if tomorrow for example everybody woke up and said Im not paying my TV license? (which should be just common sense because you are literally paying for your own brainwashing) what could they actually do? Millions of people saying no, they couldn't do anything? There is not enough cronies to enforce it! What if we all turned around and said you know what its not possible to ban Nature or a plant, particularly one with so many medicinal benefits so we are all just going to grow one anyway whether you like it or not. Again they couldn't do anything! Their power is gone completely, it is us and our OBEDIENCE that gives them all the power that they have. We keep ourselves in the prison cell.

We lack the courage and desire to disobey, we have allowed ourselves to be used and bullied around for hundreds if not thousands of years, the time has surely come to start saying no, and I don't just mean the tiny few who understand what true freedom is about and are already heading in that direction, I mean MILLIONS if not BILLIONS of people around the World. Mass civil disobedience is the ultimate solution and an expression of TRUE anarchy. Im not talking wreaking havoc and violence here either, Im just saying as I already have done previously its simply saying no. We need to reject a tyrannical system at every turn where possible. No guns or fights are needed, you don't even need to leave the house, because it starts in the mind first, and then you just stop playing the game with them and reject, reject, reject. If we can do this in huge numbers then the reality will start to change and we will start to throw down our chains. We have to understand that this system is not the powerful deity we make out it is, its actually a house of cards that if enough of us started to reject will fall down easily. Many of the problems we face have very simple solutions but they take courage, vision, and imagination to push the boundaries and dare to be something that humanity has never been before and that is quite simply to be TRULY free. All it needs is that simple two letter word 'no'. I think it was Martin Luther King who said 'One has a moral responsibility to disobey unjust laws' and not a truer sentence has ever been said in my opinion. No consent, then there is no control, control only happens when it is allowed. Its surely time to stand up and disobey laws made by immoral men who are not even playing the game themselves?

Something that shocked me was an incident where my car had been clamped. I had caused no harm or loss to any other being so in my mind I had broken no 'law' Im talking about Natural Law. Now I attempted to remove the clamp and as I was doing so a man pulled up beside me in his car whilst I was messing around underneath, and he said to me 'You shouldn't be doing that, Im going to call the police' I was dumbfounded by this. Here I was minding my own business trying to get on with daily life, when my property had been violated so I couldn't go anywhere, I ran the risk of loss of earnings through not being able to get to work if I didn't conform and cough up the 250 pounds 'release fee' and a fellow citizen, a brother in many ways, was threatening to call the authorities that would have thrown me into a cage! This was a classic example of the Stockholm syndrome mindset. Someone who LOVED his masters so much he would report other people that disobey them, protecting the very system that enslaves him! Calling out people like me who ultimately were trying to make a small stand against tyranny. It was truly unreal I was shocked to say the least, what it did was really underline the total bondage peoples minds are in, total servitude to the State. In a way Im glad it happened now, because there couldn't be a more strong example of how humans police other humans, and really the authorities have to do very little to control us. People who love their servitude so much that they will fight to protect it. Unfortunately this is where we are right now as a species, people would rather side with the enemy that make their lives so extremely difficult each day than make a stand for any kind of freedom. Like Ive said before they really have no idea about what true freedom really is, and one could argue do we really deserve it?

The laughable thing is that people think that we are somehow an evolved species, and the people at the top playing us like pawns on a chessboard must think its hilarious. They must sit around their big expensive banquets where they plan in which direction to take their slaves next and laugh so hard. I would imagine their would be fits of laughter that we keep each other in check for them, they can literally just sit back and cream off all our hard labor. This needs to end, this diseased mentality, its holding us back and frankly its downright embarrassing. People who are actually brave enough to make a stand and have found the courage to do so should be encouraged, supported, and helped in any way necessary. What that man should've done is got out of his car and lent me a hand, supported me, a siege mentality would have developed that can be built upon, and then when he needed my help one day I would have gladly returned the favor.

On a more positive note we are starting to see people come together more and more. There have been incidents where bailiffs (which God only knows could choose to do such an evil job, literally throwing poor people out onto the streets) have turned up to carry out evictions and have been met with hundreds of people supporting the evictee, which has then resulted in the eviction at least being held off for a while. Yet now the bailiffs are calling the police to assist them, the people that are supposed to support and protect the people! The police have absolutely no legal or lawful right to be there doing this, this is no more than fascism. But this is what we need to see more of, people coming together in that community spirit again, helping and supporting each other. Imagine a World where if an eviction took place and it was 50,000 people turning up in support and not 50? It wouldn't happen, again they wouldn't be able to get away with it. Yet that is the kind of level we need to get to make forward strides, it is growing slowly but surely and its important we continue on that upward curve, and to realise that we are all in this together.

# THE BIG DISCONNECT

In terms of unity and togetherness this seems to be an extremely difficult thing to garner in this day and age. It seems to me people are more concerned with staring down at their phones than they are with actually having a real life physical conversation with somebody. In many ways we are more connected than ever before for example I can be in Cambodia and make a Skype call to somebody in Colombia, this is an amazing benefit, and in so many ways the World has got smaller. But the longer it goes on I feel people are more concerned with how they live their virtual lives than they are their real ones. We are well and truly 'plugged in' technologically speaking, but spiritually we couldn't be more disconnected. Cities full of empty people staring down at their phones, its quite spooky. It seems that our addiction to technology is like a new Religion, and technology has an agenda of its own which is for another book!

This is particularly concerning when you consider our almost complete disconnect to Nature, which really does seem so irrelevant in peoples lives these days. Its scary that children know how to download apps before they learn the names of the birds and the animals in their own areas, it literally frightens me when I see kids with Ipads in their hands. Now Im no parent granted but having them cooped up all day staring at a screen cannot be good. That's without even touching on the dangers of WIFI and EMFs on the human body. We are so disconnected from Nature that the vast majority of people couldn't give a f*** what happens because its not real for them. Is it any wonder that this Planet is being absolutely annihilated when people are more concerned about chasing Pokemon? People don't care about the rainforests disappearing, or the Oceans being overfished because its got nothing to do with their online lives, and their general me, me, me attitude. Yet what are we teaching the next generations? Exactly the same is the answer, and if they are hardwired not to care either then just what generation is going to step in and take responsibility? If kids are growing up to be conditioned around technology then of course they are not going to care so much about the Natural World. Its human arrogance again, we think we can just do what we want, not take any actions ourselves, and expect to just keep up the take, take, take. Well at some point we are going to get a RUDE awakening, and I for one don't want that on my conscience and neither should you.

We are marching quickly towards another Facebook/Twitter generation, collecting 'likes' and 'comments' on selfies and pictures of our dinner whilst the World is going up in flames! What happened to kids playing? Using their imaginations? What actually happened to kids being kids? I remember as a child going down the park when the Sun came up, and I wouldn't come back until it started going down again. I know times have changed a bit but really?? That much? Maybe its just easier to give a kid an Ipad than to spend time exploring and explaining Nature, developing their love and appreciation for it. The way I see things going right now literally nobody is going to give a fuck soon. Im guilty of using social media a lot myself but that is to raise awareness more often than not.

Without Nature we have nothing, think about what Nature gives us when we are outside. It's the perfect cure for the worst of moods, it balances, and reenergises us. There has to be balance in this crazy technological age. Currently I am in Japan right now where I have just got off a train where the entire carriage were staring down at their phones. Nobody talks or is interested in connecting with each other. I actually don't know if this can even be halted, we seem to be so obsessed with it, its almost become an addiction. We see this is extremely evident when there is a new Iphone released. Here we have an exact same model as the previous phone, with a few token 'improvements' thrown in and there are people sleeping outside the shop OVERNIGHT to be the first person to buy one, paying hundreds of pounds for a few added extras in comparison to the previous model which works just fine. All this effort just so they can impress their friends who probably couldn't care less anyway!

Consumerism is the new Religion, people 'shopping until they drop' buying stuff they don't need with money they don't have. Feeding perfectly into the purposely created debt based society which enslaves them. Its no longer about morals, what you can contribute to the World, or how you can help others, no its all about how expensive your watch is, what model car you have, and how big your house is, a constant race to 'keep up with the Jones.' People paying 80% more for a t-shirt that some poor child in China was paid less than peanuts to make just because it has a Nike tick, or whatever the designer label happens to be.

These are all yet more examples of how people are looking for things outside themselves to make them feel happy and fulfilled. Materialistically we have never been richer as a society, but spiritually we are dead. The only things that can truly make a person happy is true connection to self, and that only comes with deep knowledge and soul searching, understanding our spiritual Nature and how spiritual laws operate, serving others not just the self, and finding your true purpose in life. All these things have been replaced by Gucci, Prada, and BMW. People are running away from themselves and into the arms of big corporations, because after all shopping can make you happy! We are devolving at such a rate its frightening, what has happened to us? Why are we giving ourselves over to these companies that are milking us dry? That pay no taxes? What is the obsession? People are so obsessed with how they look from the outside, they completely disregard who they are inside. The outside is just masking a deep insecurity they feel on the inside.

Have you ever noticed that there is always some kind of event to get the masses obediently out to the shops in their droves? If its not Christmas its Valentines day, Easter, or Halloween. Do people not get bored of this year after year? It's the same every year, spend, spend, spend otherwise you don't love your mother, brother, girlfriend, or wife. Its turned into one big huge guilt trip! I actually remember a time when Christmas was more about family and spending time with those you love, now its all about how much money you can spend. I was fortunate as a child to have generous parents who would treat us at Christmas, but I never got spoiled how kids do today, you know what though? It made me appreciate what I had so much more. I was glad to have that lesson of valuing and appreciating something, yet nowadays its so different kids get everything! Yet they appreciate NOTHING as parents are just teaching them to be good consumers as the cycle continues when they get older. There almost seems to be this underliying competition amongst parents too, comparing what little Johnny got to their own. Its madness, then they spend the first 6 months of the year trying to pay off their Christmas debts. What is worse is that they cannot even see how they have been duped! The big corporations bleeding them dry in the months running up to Christmas day (which now starts in September in the UK). Then the very NEXT day dropping their prices after everyone has paid FULL prices, selling goods they could have sold at half price the whole time! The people flock to the sales with the few pennies that they have left, its one big con, it has absolutely nothing to do with love or family anymore. Its about ramping up the feeding frenzy of peoples consuming habits. Make no bones these big corporations are also laughing at us.

Its one big circus and I cannot bare it, same old songs every year, same TV programs, and same queues everywhere, it's the polar opposite of what it is supposed to stand for and that's without going into detail about what that date is REALLY about, which is in relation to the winter solstice, but that is also for another book.

People are held in bondage by their very debt. I was the same at one point in my life, just going along with it all without question, although it never really felt right. We need to realise that all these dates where we are told we must spend are just huge scams, we need to stop feeding our energy and hard earned money back into these blood suckers. Or at least create something more loving and authentic. Of course I am not opposed to spending time with loved ones or expressing feelings for someone you care about, but why do we have to do it when THEY say we have to? If I want to express my love for my mother or a girlfriend I don't need the State to tell me when I should be doing it or how much I need to spend. To me these events are just yet more distractions so people don't have time to ponder their own slavery, then they actually contribute to it more by accruing more debt.

# Caging the Mind

I strongly feel that tradition, in general, massively holds humanity back, many of them are just based purely on mind control, developed and propagated by people who want more power, wealth, and control. Having been very fortunate in my life to have travelled quite extensively I see it everywhere. Take Eastern Asia for example and places like Korea and Japan. They have a deep respect for teachers, elders, or any kind of authority figure. This is all well and good if that person has EARNT that respect, but in these places it is given automatically by default. Whatever that person says or does is seen as gospel and will be obeyed without question, or blindly followed just because they hold a particular position in society. The whole region is extremely suppressed because what that does is immediately shut down any freedom of speech, reasoning, or debate. I know from teaching English to young people in that area of the World that they feel extremely frustrated and trapped, feeling forced to study certain subjects or take up certain professions that do not feed their soul just because a teacher or parent has told them that is what they should do. When I travelled to Japan I couldn't get over how obedient the place is, folk having to walk on a certain side of the pavement, or queue in a certain way for everything. I even got told off by the driver because I was talking on a night bus just after 11pm on a trip from Tokyo to Osaka!

When a culture has been developed to never question authority, or respect them regardless of if they have earnt it, then imagine how this mindset benefits those in power? We are taught from a young age to never question authority, elders, or teachers. Put down, told to shut up, punished if we dare speak out about anything. As we grow up with this indoctrination it becomes habitual. Traditions in my view, most of them anyway are poisonous, how about a new tradition or Religion based around free thinking and open mindedness? No boundaries on questioning people, and especially those in so called 'authority' not taking their word at face value. On a positive note people, and especially young people I have spoken to, are fed up with it, they're tired of being told what they should be doing all the time, and there are more and more starting to step away from this mindset. Im not saying respect is inherently wrong, but like I say it should be something that is earnt. This highlights the eternal problem humanity faces, and that is the simple lack of independent thinking, a World where we are constantly allowing others to do the thinking for us whether that be parents, governments, the television, or whoever. Its high time free thinking became a tradition, and imagine what a fantastic, interesting, and exciting that society would be to live in, instead of the billions of drones we have turned into, repeating each other all the time. Lets unleash originality, independence, individuality, creativity, and expression, the TRUE Nature of humanity that we all have in our lockers.

On the subject of oppression and the caging of individual thoughts, ideas, and concepts we have that oh so wonderful thing called 'political correctness' which completely shuts down any free and open discussion before it has even began. Is there anything these days that you're allowed to talk about without somebody getting upset? So many subjects now fall under the category of being taboo that we literally cant touch anything. Its becoming harder and harder to even talk about the very people who control us and our very lives. Ive seen it on peoples faces when you even try to approach a topic which could be deemed as somewhat controversial, its almost like 'you cant say that' is written all over their faces. For example when you bring up how many paedophiles, dead, alive, and suspected have been awarded MBEs' and knighthoods by the Queen people instantly shut down. Any discussion that could go against their rigid belief systems, and protection of the State is shut down before it even begins. The fact is that it is politics itself that is 'incorrect' but what we are able to discuss has been cleverly ring fenced off so nothing ever moves forward or gets solved.

Sometimes you have to stand back in awe of how free speech has been shut down. Even the very words 'free speech' as if ALL speech shouldn't be free in the first place?! Hidden right there in plain sight. We are cunningly fed through media what is and what is not acceptable to talk about, yet we are free to constantly spread fear and negativity about Muslims and immigrants because the TV says that is ok. Question 9/11 however and be prepared to be shut down. People have said to me I should be 'careful' in discussing certain topics, well if we REALLY did have free speech then why should it be of concern? Could it be that certain people don't want us to question certain issues? If I don't have the freedom to speak ANYTHING that happens to pop into my mind then I am definitely not free!

Take the Holocaust for example, in some Countries you can literally be thrown in prison (and people have) for just asking questions about the official version of an event that shaped our World forever. Truth does not fear questioning, ever. So why cant we debate such a historic event? Could it be that we might find holes all over what we have been told? Il leave that up to you to research. Just remember the winner always writes the history books!

For us to have freedom of speech there seems to be an awful lot of restrictions. Could it be that we are free to talk as long as its what THEY agree we can talk about? A society that lives in fear of what their government will do to them if they speak out is not a free society lets get that straight. Our ability to speak openly is eroding by the day, so we need to combat this with MORE speech, pushing the boundaries like never before. Indeed silence is a War crime in and of itself, and by staying silent we are siding with our oppressors. I know many people who are aware that things are not quite right but are too frightened to talk about anything, if this is the case then you maybe alive but the soul in you is already dead. Your soul is all about expression and if that is gone then there really is no point. We all have a purpose to fulfill in life and if we cannot speak freely, unapologetically, and stand raw in our truth then we will forever remain a slave. So then what is the point of our existence? So there we have it political correctness suppressing our mental and vocal abilities to probe and discern generating yet more mental bondage. Then we have the twin brother of course 'health and safety' which now controls our physical movements which could be a whole other book albeit a very boring one!

The other issue at hand which is extremely prominent in todays World is what the great researcher Mark Passio coined as 'emotional mind control' where everything has to FEEL good all the time, anything else is to be looked upon as 'negative' even if it might move us on consciously. No never acknowledge or talk about anything bad because people just want to hear good information all the time. Well newsflash the World isn't like that, things need to be said, negative things, things that will make you wince. Because right now that is what is required, a good honest hard look at ourselves and what we are allowing here. We have turned into a population of pansies, folk getting upset and offended at the slightest of things. I want people to get offended because I am offended, I am offended at people's lack of basic decency, their lack of care for what is happening, that offends me greatly, so if people get offended by truth then GOOD. It might rock their boat so they may actually start thinking about what their own role is in all of this.

Everything has to sound nice and fluffy or else it is just rejected out of hand. We have turned into emotional babies. When did this happen exactly? Its embarrassing. I see this no more prominent than in the 'truth movement' where a particular researchers entire work can be disregarded just because they don't like the tone in which they present or deliver something, it matters not to some of these people how TRUE what that person is saying is because the delivery or information has made them feel uncomfortable. Even if that information could be an absolute goldmine and really empower them, if it doesn't make them feel good then its thrown out of the window. Information doesn't have to FEEL good for it to be true, indeed the most beneficial and often groundbreaking information I have personally come across has often felt the exact opposite and has quite often made me feel uncomfortable. But in the long run it has increased my understanding of the World around me by leaps and bounds.

Again what this does is shut down any kind of debate and future progress before it even gets started, as we constantly look for information that just makes us feel warm and fuzzy inside. You know what? There is LOTS of that about, and in many cases it is the warm and fluffy stuff that is deceptive in Nature, particularly within the New Age movement where its all about keeping 'vibrations high', never look at the negative, and just 'accept' everything that is evil because its all just "love and light'. We will all just ride our rainbow unicorns off into the sunset! It couldn't be further from the truth, the very REASON humanity is in such a mess is because we have remained focused on the self and just accepted everything that is bad for so long. Everyone is looking for that dopamine hit all the time, that little buzz to make them feel better, ok fair enough I get that, its nice to feel good, but maybe if we got our shit together then we would feel good ALL of the time!

A truly evolved society looks at all information regardless of how it makes them feel. That is symbolic of a wise society, as it realizes that a lot of solutions are actually found by looking at the negatives, certainly not ignoring them or disregarding them because they make us feel uncomfortable. When did any real positive long lasting change come in your own life without looking at your bad habits or behavioral patterns? There are issues on this Planet that aren't very nice right now which require our urgent attention, we need to look at these issues for the sake of future generations to come. We need to grow up. What we are dealing with here is no joke, it takes courage and discernment. We need to face the challenges head on no matter how painful and upsetting to be able to transcend them into positives.

We are losing ourselves and our grip on reality with what I call 'fake positivity' it literally drives me around the bend. Don't get me wrong Im all for a positive attitude, but not at the price of ignoring reality. These fakers go around pretending everything is amazing and that just by 'thinking positive thoughts' everything will end up great. Well try asking those in Gaza, Syria, or homeless people on the streets how that is working out for them. We need to be positive yes, but POSITIVELY address the negatives that require our urgent attention, not bury our heads in the sand in a World that is crying out for us to do something about the situation. We can do all the 'love and light' stuff after we have sorted out the war, famine, and poverty!

It's complete fakeness people burying both their own problems and World issues, masking what is really going on and living in la la land. Problems will continue to get worse on both an individual and collective level unless they are addressed. I love the saying from my Essex roots 'you cannot polish a turd' there are probably a million better ways to express the same thing but I like to cut to the chase! True happiness cannot be found until we resolve our own internal conflicts, and the same is true on a wider scale. My honest assessment with how things stand right at this moment in time is that humanity is a group of weak cowards, living in absolute fear of doing or saying something that may offend someone else or a group of people. Particularly men, what has happened to men? Supposedly we are here to be the protectors of the females and children. Yet I know men who are aware of the situation and do absolutely zero. Is it any wonder that females feel unsafe in this World and look to the State for safety and security? To be a man these days is quite embarrassing to be honest.

Another huge mind hack which has been cleverly manipulated by the ruling class is that of those two words 'conspiracy theorist' has there ever been any two words in the history of the Planet that have ever been so powerful in shutting down discussion and debate before it even starts? Apparently anyone who questions the actions of blatantly known liars falls into this bracket, anyone who questions the official version of something might also be known as a 'tin foil hat wearer' Because governments and people in power NEVER lie do they? No instead of being mature, looking at things with an open heart and mind lets beat people down immediately they threaten our prescious slave World view. The truth is EVERYBODY should be a conspiracy theorist! Why is it so outlandish for somebody to interrogate those that make decisions that effect our everyday lives? Its just another extension of Stockholm syndrome as I mentioned earlier, folk wanting to protect the people that oppress them.

Lets take for example 'Weapons of mass destruction' in Iraq where over one million people were killed, was that all a conspiracy when they didn't find any? These are the same people that told us that a few Muslims sitting in a cave managed to corrupt the most protected airspace in the World on 9/11, so we should just take all that at face value then? As I say all it does it shuts down debate which only ever benefits the tiny few. Ironically many, many events that were once considered 'conspiracy' have gone on to be proven lies by governments so why is it so far fetched? Interestingly enough the term was first coined by the CIA at the time of the Kennedy assassination because people were starting to ask too many questions, it was used to demonise people who were thinking for themselves as whackos or nut jobs. That story also stinks to high heaven also so I would encourage people to independently research that one too. Just check out his speech before he was murdered where he was attempting to expose the hidden hands and shadow governments operating behind World events pulling the strings. The REAL controllers who lurke in the background pulling the strings of the puppet politicians who are there only to give you the ILLUSION of choice

These people are bought and paid for by the REAL decision makers . Give the peasants a vote every four years and they will think they have choice and freedom. Why do you think nothing ever changes no matter who you vote for? Its simply because the people behind the agenda stay the same, and they don't want things to change! Red corner versus blue corner, Corbyn versus Cameron, left versus right, Liberals versus Conservatives, all constructs that on the face of it look like they are pitting off against each other but in reality they are all patting each others backs in the Parliamentary or Congress bars afterwards. Does anyone ever question how strange it is that former British Prime Minister David Cameron is fourth cousin to the Queen? Or out of 330 million people in America the best presidential candidates that they can come up with are Donald Trump and Hilary Clinton? This is 'choice' apparently.

When are the likes of you and I ever going to have a chance to run our Country? The answer is NEVER. As the great George Carlin once said 'It's a big club and you and I aint in it'! A club which in the UK sees an overwhelming majority of Prime Ministers all coming from one school which is Eton, it's a literal training ground! Where are the candidates from my old school in Essex or your town wherever you may be? Lets get one thing straight, Presidents and Prime Ministers are LONG since chosen before people go to the ballot boxes on election day. Carefully hand picked to tickle the masses fancy. Always a good cop and a bad cop, one that on the surface SAYS they are ready to make harsh changes to 'improve' the Country, and the other which wears that innocent mask of kindness, or relates to the common man. Yet what happens when they get into power? More lies, War crimes, and tax evasion. Every election without fail, people getting stirred up into a frenzy to give their power away to another wolf in sheep clothing. Yet try expressing this to the average person and you are a 'conspiracy theorist' Even when ballot papers go missing , no its all one big conspiracy.

It's one big joke and we wonder why we find ourselves in the position we are in, we cannot even have an honest, frank, and open debate without shouting each other down. This is an EVIL term, it literally locks down our very consciousness. You may aswell be involved in organized Religion if everything around you is going to be written off as a conspiracy theory at the drop of a hat. Is it just the Stockholm syndrome playing out here or rather a deep underlying fear that if they have to acknowledge the World is different to what they have been told then they may have to change themselves or do something about it? Its so much easier to just believe the lies isn't it? The funny thing is people are constantly saying how we need to be truthful and that they want the truth yet in reality it seems they LOVE the lies, they love being fed bullshit day after days. No its much easier to be stuck in a monumental amount of bullshit that we are living in and pretend everything is ok.

If I am a conspiracy theorist then I am dam proud of it because it means that I actually have an open mind. Im not saying that every theory is true either, there is a lot of disinformation out there, but at the very minimum at least I investigate all angles. I can critically think and I am not just another sheep in the sheep pen waiting to go to be slaughtered. EVERYONE should be a conspiracy theorist as I have said! Its time to put those words to bed once and for all as the absolute farcical term it is and realise it benefits nobody, only those that want more control and power. Surely basic logic can tell us that this is a term cleverly crafted and coined by those that don't want us delving into things we shouldn't be delving into? Of course because the truth is a real threat to their existence.

I find people also use this term a lot when they have no real argument in a subject matter or when they have no real leg to stand on. It's like the fail safe term for those who feel threatened by the truth to fall back on. When people who have watched a 10 minute 'news' bulletin come across someone who has done hours and hours of extensive research which can blow the official version away, what easier way to discredit a whole argument by the use of the 'conspiracy theorist' jibe? Its so weak and all it really reveals is a completely uneducated point of view.

Take the Military for example you can tell them until you are blue in the face that the UK/US governments have admitted funding terrorist organisations, information which would really put their whole World view into question, and indeed their own service. No its written off immediately as a conspiracy, no real interest in truth or REAL freedom, which is highly concerning considering they will be going to kill and bomb people at some point. No the only interest is protecting the lie, even at the cost of other innocent people's lives!

So it should be clear by now how human beings shut each other down and police themselves even before a basic discussion can get started, using terms that thwart forward thinking and freedom of expression. The solution is simple and its about growing up again, as I have said a wise society would encourage debate and different view points not shut each other down. This needs to be encouraged not ridiculed. Basic questioning of what we are being told should be the absolute bare minimum that we should strive for, especially that what we are being told is coming directly from liars, surely people know that by now. Free thinking is hanging by a literal thread as we continue the march towards non thinking robots, where everybody has the same opinion on everything.

# Groomed for Servitude

This suppression of expression of course starts at a very young age, literally as soon as we leave the womb we are told what is right and wrong, true and untrue, we have teachers that we have to 'obey' and there is discipline involved for anyone who questions them. So right from the start we are learning to submit to authority figures. Personally I couldn't wait to leave school, I found most subjects boring, repetitive, and I felt like I was going into a prison everyday, which is really basically just what they are, you even have the big steal gates that are locked up to keep you inside! Subjects we are taught in school are in the main completely irrelevant to when you grow up into adulthood. There is no knowledge of self passed down, how the mind works, no mention of Universal law, or even how to be happy. Were you ever taught how to grow your own food, or how REAL health is achieved through good diet? No neither was I but I was taught things like algebra, home economics, and Religion. I was definitely taught how my opinion didn't matter, and that I should just keep quiet throughout.

Even subjects that could be viewed as beneficial are the systems version of everything, take history for example we were not taught how the British went to Australia and Native America and slaughtered the indigenous people there, or the time we went to

India and massacred people there too? I don't remember being taught that Hitler actually offered several surrenders and ceasefires to the allies in WW2 to stop it from escalating? In 'science' I didn't learn about quantum physics and that how everything is energy vibrating at different speeds to make things appear as solid? Imagine that, in school learning that everything is energy, our thoughts, emotions, and actions, and by controlling and harnessing them we can actually change our own realities? Where was the encouragement of our imagination or our creativity these hugely powerful abilities that are inherent in us all and are the very fundamental aspects to our being? What of the great Nicola Tesla who discovered free energy which is still being suppressed to this day? No we get given Edison and the light bulb. You think they don't have this technology? You think they're not sitting on it all to keep us relying on fossil fuels? Then you really need to do some research. What of that terrible plant cannabis? I had to learn for myself the hugely powerful healing qualities that plant has, surely something as unique as that would be taught in our schools? No the opposite is true, it is completely demonized.

It's their version of everything and if you repeat their version well enough then you will be rewarded with good grades or a degree. Could this be to what grade or degree you have been indoctrinated to? Are they telling us something there? I think they most certainly are, a pat on the back from the system for being a good future unquestioning slave. The creativity and imagination is being literally beaten out of kids at such a young age. Look at art in schools these days its almost non existent, funding has been cut heavily across the board. What they are doing is systematically trying to shut down the right side of the brain which encourages free thinking, creativity, and expression.

These things do not benefit the system that wants to maintain it's control. On the contrary it is the more rigid, skeptical, obedient left side of the brain that they want people locked into, so this is not just by chance. The left brain obident Daily Mail reader types are the ones they want children to grow up into. Folk who grow up spouting the systems take on reality, worker bees for the State.

Do kids really suffer from all these behavioral problems like autism, or are they just down right bored, bored with repeating the same old things day after day? Is it not that these children are just not dying to be, well children? Then there is the homework, as if being at prison all day wasn't enough they want to make sure the indoctrination infests any free fun time they may have too! Surely childhood is all about imagination, creating, playing, developing a more holistic brain where the right and the left side work in harmony and in unison. Im not saying that there should be no more academic subjects but it is so lopsided.

What is really concerning is that the State wants more and more control of the kids, longer hours at school have been suggested, fines are a regular punishment for parents who want to take their OWN children out of school in term time for a holiday! HELLO this is not right! The State does not OWN your children! Now Im even hearing of school sleepovers which is really creepy, and as I have said any free time left is being used up with more and more homework like their poor days haven't been structured enough!

Yet so many think this is normal, they cannot see that schools are nothing but prisons in both the literal sense and that of the mind, a place where instead of encouraging unity and teamwork they are taught to compete. Who can get the best grades to put them ahead of the next kid so when they leave the prison they will get ahead of the next kid in the rat race and the next prison called work. To think that they have actually managed to make homeschooling illegal in places such as Sweden, expect to see the same thing in your Country soon. Same with vaccinations in Australia where you can expect to lose any State benefits that you're entitled to if you do not vaccinate, even though there are horrific studies coming out questioning their side effects, nothing to see here all completely normal.

Who are these people that think that we have no rights to educate our children or make decisions about their health? Who do they think they are penalizing us financially for taking our children on holidays? For a family to go away in the school holidays is extremely expensive, I have even heard that soon airport securities are going to have the right to stop people from travelling if their children are supposed to be at school. What is going on here, who is the parent in this dynamic? Yet this is exactly what they want, more control of the kids so the State becomes God. A break up of the family unit where both dad and now mum are at work most of the day because its so difficult financially for them not to be, break up the family unit which allows less of a perhaps 'conscious' upbringing which is a danger to people in power. This needs to stop, parents desperately need to intervene as this gets more and more out of hand by the day. They need to stand together against these fines, and new perverted control systems coming in stealing our childrens futures. Its getting more and more inappropriate. Again I take a deep sigh when I see most parents mainly completely oblivious, Ive seen parents celebrate when their child gets accepted into a certain prison over another. It's just more giving our power away again, allowing others to educate our young, and it goes on generation after generation. One era of obedient robots hand the baton to the next era of obedient robots, a constant churning out of willing, unquestioning State repeaters ready to pay their taxes and 'support the troops' in the next War. No wonder it goes on generation after generation because nobody ever wants to come in and buck the trend, where is the glitch in the Matrix?

I'm not saying here that all teachers are bad either, their intent is good, they no doubt love kids and want to help them in their development, the problem is that they are just repeating to the children what they learnt to repeat themselves. Of course learning a foreign language or English is essential but these can be homeschooled. Some will say that most people don't have the time or the money to that, well this is going to sound harsh but surely these things should be thought and planned out before taking the massive decision to bring a child into this World? Personally I would want the absolute best for my child, and the thought of packing them off to prison each day would kill my soul.

I'm under no illusion how unpopular this will sound but is it true? Absolutely. Its clear to me that homeschooling is the way forward here, people will argue that kids wouldn't be able to socialize and would somehow be 'withdrawn' from society, I just see that as weak excuses to be honest. There are lots of clubs, activity groups, sports teams available in local communities these days. I couldnt think of anything more amazing, and what a gift to the World it would be to raise a free thinking, creative, holistic brained child up, to teach them about Nature (where is the lesson on that in schools?) deep knowledge of self that will empower them for the rest of their lives, or even just teach them what it means to be a good moral person in a World where everyone is out for themselves. Its exciting when I think about how different society would be if children we being bought up in a conscious manner, they already carry with them so much wisdom into the World and it gets completely lost through constant indoctrination from all angles. Again the choice is ours we can either raise another generation of robots subjected to a life of conformity, or we can bring up a generation of fully rounded spiritual powerhouses who then have a great chance of creating a better future not only for themselves but for their own children.

I really feel for the younger generations, they even have to pay for their own indoctrination at university and then come out realizing that there are barely any jobs. They start adult life with a chain of debt already around their necks. How can they even begin to pay off these debts when there are no jobs? How is this a good start in life? More importantly why are parents not thinking about this before encouraging their young to spend another four years of their valuable lives and God knows how much money just for a pat on the back from the State? Again Im being harsh on parents, and I understand the difficulties and how hard it must be in many ways, but in all seriousness I don't see that much concern about these issues from them, its not even a problem for most? Its just again what we have always done. They seem quite ok with the State dominating their children, I don't have kids so people could argue that 'I will never know' Well I can assure you there is no way on Earth I would let these things just slide, no way I don't let these things slide in my own personal life let alone if I was one day lucky enough to have my own wonders of creation. I feel many parents, of course not all, are just lazy. There I said it, tell me that's not true? Show me parents that in their droves are standing up to the State, are questioning vaccinations, are giving their children a choice over whether or not they eat dead animals? Parents don't even seem to care about the poisons in things like McDonalds or the amount of cancer causing sugar in all the food. No I don't see it, and Im not backing down on this opinion because in the main it is 100% true.

So from the early indoctrination I have spoken about where we are pitted up against each other from day one, competing to be the best, and focusing on the self only, of course this then plays out when they finally get out of the schooling system and into adult life, into the wonderful World of capitalism and greed where these early lessons come in very handy as we enter the 'rat race'. Do people ever wonder why its called a race, or the human race? Funny that, could it be because that is exactly what it is by chance? A race against each other, rushing to reach certain career milestones which spiritually mean absolutely nothing. Collecting material trinkets along the way which will keep you looking outside yourself for happiness which can only ever be found within. First it's the new watch, then the car, then the apartment, and then the house, just one thing after another as you keep on treading water. Just one more hurdle and I will be happy and fulfilled, one more promotion, then onto the next one. This race, is nothing more than a trap.

Most people know deep down this isn't right, surely we weren't put on this Earth to work until we drop? Yet the hours are getting longer, more is expected of us, and for less pay. The way we are treated by many of these companies is nothing short of just a number. I know I have been there myself, I did it for far too long. Working all the hours Gods sends because somehow youre not 'committed' if you don't! I was absolutely exhausted, stressed, and in my mid 30s felt that if I didn't find another way of living I knew I would be well on my way to an early grave. My creativity was completely stunted and of course I had no time to even discover that side of me. At the weekends where I had been sufficiently 'weakened' I was too tired to do anything. I didn't even know I could write.

Fifty to sixty hours a week stressed, all to hit meaningless targets which only ever served the big CEOs. Five days on, two days off, week after week, month after month, and year after year, working for companies that couldn't give a dam about me personally, it was all about the bottom line, and what numbers I was bringing in. My life was just a reflection of what billions of people go through daily, I was no different. With the way the global economy is and the general lack of jobs these companies can replace you at the drop of the hat, which is why they can now get away with such poor treatment of their staff. Try taking a day off sick these days without being made to feel guilty!

Interestingly enough when I was travelling in Japan I would speak to people who who just take one week off a year! The commuter trains were packed like sardines where there are actually people employed to PUSH and squeeze people into carriages, imagine that every morning when you have just got out of bed. Then whilst taking trains through cities at night it was not uncommon to see many people still working in their offices at 10 or 11pm still. This is supposed to be 'living' this is nothing more than existing, and there is a huge difference between the two words.

What really gets me is the whole glorification of work, and how people are so proud of being 'busy' all the time, they wear it like a badge of honor! 'Oh I cant talk right now Im busy' or 'Im so busy with this project the next few weeks'. It's the same when you meet someone for the first time and they ask 'what do you do for a living?' REALLY is that what you want to know about me? What I do to earn fake pieces of paper to put food on the table and a roof over my head? How about what are you creating right now? What is your purpose? What makes you feel alive? What is the most amazing thing you have done? That's what I want to know about people, I want to know their soul, what makes them tick, the REAL them, not about their 9-5 existence. Yet people love to talk about their jobs, probably because that's where they spend the majority of their lives sadly.

We just love to glorify our own slavery, this is particularly prominent with people when you mention taxes. How often have you seen and heard people when they talk about how 'they have paid their taxes all their lives' what you basically mean is you've been robbed by the State continuously for years with the threat of violence and imprisonment if you don't automatically hand over a large chunk of your hard earned wages each month. And that the very people demanding this of you are paying little to no taxes themselves, and spending your tax money on War and weapons to blow up innocent people in far away lands! Wow really something to be proud of. When really it should be something that we are all disgusted with, what youre basically saying is that you have been a good, diligent slave your whole entire life and have allowed yourself to be robbed by immoral people.

I'm not saying that we shouldn't contribute to society financially but it should be voluntary, your choice, and certainly not under the threats of violence. Of course I am talking about a more evolved society here, in the current 'whats in it for me' level of consciousness it probably wouldn't work so well. But as we raise in consciousness, that I would hope at least, would bring more wisdom, where everyone would play ball with that idea. I don't have all the absolute answers, Im just throwing ideas into the melting pot, all I know is that the way it is set up currently is very wrong and only serves to benefit the tiny few who can just raise taxes whenever they like and cream off the top. They are coming after the middle class now too, reports as I write this that newly elected President Donald Trump, the so called savior, is now talking about raising taxes which will have a massive impact on an already struggling working class American population who, once again, put their blind faith in this parasite who has already dropped a whole load of bombs on Syria and his term has barely started!

Like I say Im trying open people's minds here and help them realise what has happened to them, we can work on the solutions once we have acknowledged that there is a problem. I think in the future we may see perhaps a new crypto currency, or perhaps even a bartering system where we still function, and hopefully thrive. Again its down to the imagination and what we perceive human beings can achieve. The current monetary and taxation system has its tentacles around our throats. Alternative ways carries risk yes, but the rewards would far outweigh that in the long run. Im also not saying here that we shouldn't work at all either, but not like this, not when we are so stressed out to the maximum. Our physical bodies are not designed to work so hard. I imagine a good civilized society would work maybe a three or four day week, we cannot continue like this surely? Not if we are seriously thinking about evolving to anything greater, even if that might be a minority right now.

We're so much more than worker bees for the so called elite, carrying out all the jobs they don't want to do themselves. Can we really expect to be truly happy being woken up by an alarm at 6.30am, rushed into the shower, then straight into commuter traffic on the way to a job to earn money for somebody who doesn't even care about you? Of course this doesn't apply to every single person or employee out there, and if you have found a job you love doing then great, I feel that is the ultimate aim where we make work our passion in life so it doesn't even feel like working. We do it because we want to do it and not because we have to. I have to generalize this point because it is true for billions of people. That Sunday dread feeling of going into work the next day, I was even very sensitive to that as a child and I remember feeling uneasy on Sundays, I obviously didn't even work at the time I wasn't old enough, but maybe I was picking up on the collective fear energy of a looming Monday morning?

The solution must surely lie in not accepting this as our lot in life, and also developing the will and desire to want our lives to be more about living and less about existing. I think as a collective we are so downtrodden and tired of it being this way that people do not have the energy to even start thinking about change. I understand that, especially if you have children and bills to pay. But things will only change if each and everyone of us says enough is enough. Otherwise all we are doing is ensuring our children will experience the same fate. Each generation has a moral obligation in their timeframe to ensure the next generation has a higher pedestal to stand on. Indeed in Native American culture they used to think in terms of seven generations ahead, this generation barely thinks of itself! This has not happened enough in previous eras, things have been left to slide and look at the mess that has been left. Well I don't know about you but I want to help end this once and for all. I want to be part of the beginning of a change never seen before on this Planet, the time is right because people have had enough. That excites me and it should you, just to be able to look at any child I may have in the future right between the eyes and say to myself that I did everything I could to make their World a better and brighter place would mean everything to me. If I can say that at the end of my days then I will be a happy man.

Yet for so many that thought hasn't even crossed their minds, and some of these people do have children and grandchildren, its much easier to just ignore everything and pretend things aren't on the slide because that then excuses them from taking any action. Well to those people you DO have a moral obligation to fulfill, you can call me arrogant for saying that but it's the truth whether you want to hear that or not. Who are we again as human beings to allow this on our watch? People need to get angry about this situation, and transcend that anger into positive action to effect change. We are all those ripples in that pond, how is your ripple? Have you even cast the stone out yet?

Capitalism, corporatism, and competitivism has now plunged us into a World which couldn't be more symbolic than in the TV show 'the Apprentice'. For me this epitomizes to a tee the society we have today, people who do not care or have feelings towards others just as long as they reach the top of the corporate ladder. Many will say or do anything for the chance to earn those precious slave notes, even if it means stomping all over their fellow colleagues, friends, or co workers, anything goes in the World of business. It doesn't matter how immoral the deed, if it means extracting more money then its all fair game. Trust me I saw this first hand within estate agency. Any kind of behavior can be explained away in just two words 'its business' just like the military term as I have mentioned 'collateral damage'. All cons, scams, and rip offs can be excused by just those words. Makes no difference who is robbed, harmed, deceived if its business then its all ok.

What this does to people is turn them into cold, ruthless, uncompassionate literal psychopaths. Again the sick thing is its all glorified again. Everything has a price and even our souls apparently when we sell them to the devil of corporate greed. We have become a population of 'takers' we take from each other, from the vulnerable, the elderly, and especially when it comes to Nature, which is now just seen as one giant dollar bill.

This mindset needs to be explained for what it really is and it will shock many people. This mentality is Satanic that is literally what Satanism is, all about me, what can I get, I don't care who I hurt to get what I want etc. Satanism is a way of life serving only the self, its not some devil in the bowels of hell. Satanism is a way of being in the World where people also believe there are no consequences for their actions, so ask yourself this how many people around you are practicing Satanism in their daily lives? The sad truth is that the vast majority of human beings are Satanists and they don't even realise it. We have adopted the very mindsets of the people that rule over us, this is their belief system we have taken on as shocking as it sounds, a parasitical life form on this Planet.

# THE COMMODITY THAT IS NATURE

The corporate capitalist era that we live in is intertwined with our very home and her resources, the Planet and Nature are as I have said, seen nothing more than something we can extract and rape for cash. Harvesting all her resources on a daily basis, fracking the land, spilling oil into the oceans, and cutting down her lungs in the rainforests, the list goes on. Just how long are we going to be allowed to treat her this way until there are dire consequences for us all? Im not fear mongering here, I'm being absolutely realistic. There surely is only a certain amount of time before our mother finally shakes us off like the fleas we have become? We show her no real love or care so we shouldn't be surprised if one day we get whats coming to us. In a way maybe that wouldn't be such a bad thing. I feel sorry for the animals, sea life, plants, and trees, to co exist with a species that wants to destroy and take all the time it must be a living hell! Even the more untouched places have no place to hide from mankind as I am seeing first hand here in Asia. It is extremely apparent here that the new uprising, power, and wealth coming from China is having a huge impact on this part of the World. Beautiful coastlines, and almost deserted Islands of Cambodia and Vietnam are being annihilated for restaurants, hotels, casinos, and golf courses, its tragic. All this is going completely unchecked by these government as they take a nice little back hander, meanwhile the average Cambodian lives on less than one dollar a day. Of course this is seen as a good thing by the locals as it brings in more tourists, job opportunities, and money in general so its allowed to go on completely unchecked. This is just a reflection of what seems to be going on everywhere on the Planet it seems.

Ultimately the Planet will be fine in the long run, we are the ones that are expendable, its just we are too arrogant to believe that could happen, we are too busy acting like the Gods that we think we are. There are people out there that truly believe we are the highest form of intelligence here. Seriously that really is one big joke and couldn't be any further from the truth, and like I say the rude awakening is just around the corner if we don't wake up sooner or later. Again I quote George Carlin when he summed it up perfectly and said 'the Planet is fine, the people are fucked' and there was the other famous Native American quote 'Only when all the oceans and forests have been destroyed, will we realise that we cant eat money'.

As I sit here writing this looking out along the Cambodian coastline just thinking how amazingly beautiful our Planet is, and how incredibly lucky we are to be able to call this place our home. Yet we have bastardised her and prostituted her for money. People in suits driving fast cars with expensive homes have used her and we have just allowed this to happen completely unchecked. Then when the tiny few do try and make a stand you have the good old 'order followers' standing in the way again, protecting corporate interests over what is essentially the people attempting to protect their very home!

At this time the huge protests are taking place against the Dakota pipeline, this is being built on sacred Native American lands which carry huge risks to the environment and the potential poisoning of local water supplies. It could have terrible consequences for millions of people. Encouragingly there are many people protesting and trying to protect the land from being raped. Yet we have the police, who by the way are dressed in full military outfits and driving what are essentially tanks, beating and firing rubber bullets on people just trying to do the right thing which will HELP their children and grandchildren! So these drones are protecting the corporations. How can anybody who is not a psychopath fire on their own people for wanting to protect the land?? So again who is the REAL problem here the people who want to extract the Earth to line their own pockets or the people that are enabling this to happen by following orders? It is again the system protectors that are ensuring this happens, they don't think that this is THEIR water too! It would be interesting to see what they would say to their young if something happened because of what they enforced one day in the future. How proud they must be with themselves at the end of their working day! Yet people want to let them off the hook all the time 'yes but they joined to help people' or 'they are just doing what they are told'. The longer people keep making excuses for this kind of immoral behavior the longer it will continue. I honestly feel that if people want to keep serving this system then they need to be isolated from society, isolated by us. How else will they realise what they are doing is wrong if we keep supporting them? No they need to FEEL this from us. The door is open for them to come and join the good fight but until that point for me personally I don't want anything to do with them.

People will say that we need a police force and military etc Ok then what are they doing about the rife child abuse going on in governments and higher? What are the police doing about that and the politicians with off shore accounts in tax havens whilst the rest of us mere mortals grind to the bone? The ones strting illegal wars, and lobbying with the weapons industry? The answer is a big fat NOTHING, as I have said they are protecting and serving them not us. It's not right and there are just no excuses anymore, and frankly Im tired of hearing them. Have a police force by all means but at least have them serving and protecting the people and the land, they should be used much like the fire brigade, called out when needed. Not out there on the streets taking away peoples rights and freedoms, and extracting money through petty fines, and shutting down demonstartions fro good people trying to protect our freedoms and the Planet. Go back into the station and don't come out until there is an actual murder, mugging or something. If we have to have a military at home to 'defend our shores' then STAY there, don't go and INVADE other places, leave people the fuck alone!

So if we are to have a future on this Planet before we get thrown in the bin as a desperate failed race, a mere embarrassment to the rest of creation we need to realise that Nature can have her say at any time, we have to stop treating her as a tool to make money, and ultimately those who want to fight to protect her should be supported and protected. We need to treat her like we treat our own mother, with love, respect, and care.

We can all make small improvements, myself included, Im not professing to be perfect when it comes to self sustainability, although I have made the single most biggest impact one person can make on the environment by going vegan which most wont want to even consider. The fact is animal agriculture is the number one cause of destruction here, acres and acres of rainforest, woodland, and forest being hacked down to make way for cattle farming and crops to grow grain for them. The Worlds Oceans, predicted to be almost fishless by 2040 due to overfishing to try to sustain a growing population, the list goes on. The most simple thing a person can do to contribute yet most don't want to hear that most uncomfortable of truths. When people say they want to help the environment, its always in their actions that shows how serious they are. The fact is people who SAY they are all for a greener way of living are still supporting its downfall by choosing to eat death, destruction, and violence. We don't need it, we thrive without it, and so would the Planet. Lets see who is REALLY serious about change, and is willing to make the necessary sacrifice?

I say to people who may be reading this who are either directly or indirectly involved in a profession or business where the destruction of Nature is involved, this is the home of your children, what are you going to tell them when they are older and the environment has been destroyed? That you were part of that?

We don't have to stay in immoral jobs, personally I'd rather have my conscience intact than extra zeros in my bank account. What would the government do if there was nobody to frack the land or to cut down the rainforests? You think they would do that hard work themselves? Of course not. Again therein lies both the problem and the solution. It comes back down to taking personal responsibility for our actions, and whilst there is a big fat pay cheque at the end of the month, who cares if we don't have a home to live on in the future?

Where does this lack of care come from? I say its down to the lack of care for ourselves and self love, I say that we are projecting pain onto the Planet that we are holding within ourselves and our own hearts. Look at the now notorious 'Black Friday' which is symbolic of the consumerist society we live in, where you have so called human beings willing to punch others in the head over a discounted TV set, the very appliance that will brainwash their own minds! Of the huge potential we have, and all that untapped creative ability is this the best we can do? Consumer slaves buying just for the sake of it. The zombie apocalypse was not some outlandish prediction, its already here, and its here to stay unless we start paying attention, the devolution of our species is quickening at a frightening pace, and with parents teaching their young to also find happiness in consuming its hard to see how this can be stopped.

If there is one day in the calendar year that epitomizes where we are right now it is that of Black Friday. How about we boycott these events? Imagine the stores opening up their doors and not a solitary soul turning up? What about if we hijacked Black Friday and went out to feed the homeless instead? I guarantee folk would feel much better about themselves doing that rather than spending $100 on a microwave for a quick dopamine hit. Id love to see the end of these multinational parasitic companies in my lifetime. Like any parasite though it can only survive if the host does nothing to stop it. As long as you keep on shopping that suits the ruling class just fine. The chains we are bound to are not locked and bolted around our ankles they are attached to Visa,

Mastercards, and store cards, these are the chains of the 21st century. A conveyor belt of obedient workers, who then need to work even harder to pay off the unnecessary debt they have accrued, who then don't even have time to ponder on their own existence. Just sitting in front of the mind numbing black box in their living room being told what else they should buy next to make them happy.

The solution has to be to start boycotting these events, start realizing that material gain doesn't equate to spiritual gain or happiness. All these consumers are ultimately doing is running away from their own shadows and deep unhappiness gaining temporary reprieve. As well as boycotting these huge bloodsuckers we need to support small businesses, which are quite often more ethical. Encouragingly there are more and more of these popping up all over the place, particularly when it comes to food stores. "Food' as these supermarkets have the cheek to call it these days can barely even be classed as that, this is an entire topic in itself. As I have said many of the solutions lie in saying no and rejecting what we have accepted as normal in our ignorance and apathy. These places will only cease to exist, as will consumerism as a whole, until we reject it in enough numbers. It is again through our aquiessence which gives the machine its strength, nobody is at fault except us. They supply what we demand, look at the huge increase in organic food, and vegan products like cheese, huge demands which are now having to be supplied by these companies. We vote with our wallets, so the question is what are you voting for?

Stop buying shit you don't need, and let's stop encouraging our kids that endlessly consuming is normal. Everything else in Nature takes the minimum of what it needs, so why should humans be any different? This is living in harmony, and as we reject more of this then perhaps the strain on our mother Earth will be eased considerably as we become more conscious beings who learn to tread carefully on our home. It might be a long way off but I imagine that we can live like this one day. There are small encouraging signs as a lot of these corporations are starting to lose money hand over fist and are now having to close stores. Organisations like McDonalds for example as people are waking up to the poisons in their menu, and are like I say, voting with their wallets. I see this trend continuing on an upward curve, that in itself is exciting and we just need to make sure it continues.

Ironically this mass addiction to all things material actually feeds into to the 'scarcity society' that we exist in as I mentioned earlier. Just enough to see them through the month, just enough to afford to eat and a roof over the head, and maybe that two week holiday a year. Pounding that treadmill harder and harder as food prices and the general cost of living goes up, but the wages stay the same. The middle class who were once sitting comfortably, briefly looking over their Daily Mail newspapers at the rest of the World, are now starting to feel the pinch. It must be so tough for families these days, but the point is nobody is asking the question why?

Why do we live in such scarcity in a World with so much abundance? Nature provides so much there should never be any kind of lack. Look at Africa and the sheer amount of minerals and resources it has, its staggering that there are people starving to death in a continent that should be absolutely thriving, yet it has been on its knees for decades? The hypocrisy of the west once again is staggering, the very people that raped that land and caused all this poverty launching campaigns such as 'Feed the World'. Funny how there is always money for War but never the poor though. Just one month that the US government spends on the military could solve the poverty crisis in Africa. So why isn't that being done? So many questions and not enough answers.

We have to come away from thinking that society is like this by chance but not by design. Scarcity mind control keeps people in fear day after day. Fear of running out and not having enough. When you come from a place of fear the idea of challenging that system that feeds your daily scraps becomes even more frightening, people associate it with biting the hand that feeds you (even though its peanuts). What if the scraps dry up? Yet why does it have to even be scraps? Others don't live off scraps, those who make the decisions of course. We're conditioned to just have enough to get by that we cannot even imagine a life of abundance. Could it be that people on a subconscious level have such a low opinion of themselves that they feel that they don't deserve it?

There are people that set these food and energy prices, the movers and shakers the REAL power players who are ensuring its more for them and less for everyone else. Work them to the bone so they are too exhausted to work out what is going on. This is what makes consumerism even more crazy in that people are under this scarcity mindset yet continue to buy more and live beyond their means. So again who is really to blame here? Is it the people setting the prices that dictate the amount of abundance available to the masses, or is it the masses themselves who never hold the people dictating to account and demand better, I would go one further and say we should stop looking for dictators altogether because it never works out well.

We are the cause of our own downfall in so many ways, once again greed, lack of care, and general apathy guarantees that we are fully taken advantage of. I sound like a broken record but it always comes back to that one issue, people need to start giving a fuck! The system has been cleverly set up to suit the system and its been allowed to happen pretty much unchecked. I would say that at this point in time if we are to want a more abundant World for ourselves then we are going to have to work for it, we have to earn it and undo hundreds of years of apathy and ignorance. The positives are that in terms of the general numbers we are in the majority compared to the people making the decisions, but people need to wake up and smell the coffee before its too late.

# THE DISEASE OF CONVENIENCE

Through our own laziness we have allowed these big corporations the monopoly on everything that we rely on, we have become way too reliant on the system to provide for us. What happens one day if there is a food shortage? It wouldn't be the first time. Look at the mass hysteria when there is a petrol shortage, folk queuing up for miles outside petrol stations to stock up on gasoline. Think about it if you were living in a large City like London or New York and there was a food shortage. What would you do? This isn't fear mongering these are real questions that we need to consider. If we are willing to hand over all control of our basic needs to people who have questionable agendas at best, then we need to be sure that they are going to have our backs in times of trouble. Look at what is happening currently in the Middle East China, Russia, Iran, and America all puffing chests out around Syria, what if it was to kick off there and the World was plunged into another World War. If you research into this you will see there are many people unbelievably that want another World War. If we were to learn how to grow our own food then if this was to happen then we would be able to cope.

I believe a huge part of the solution is that we have to become more self reliant and self sufficient, to start stepping away from others providing for us and start providing for ourselves. We have to go back to basics, back to how Nature intended life to be. Im not suggesting everyone goes 'off grid' that is not accessible for most people of course, but we should at least consider the possibility that one day we may be forced to provide for ourselves and that the nanny state may not be there to hold our hands any longer. This is certainly an area I need to work on myself. To be able to start growing food ourselves, or at least have access to somebody who does is empowering and a middle finger up to the system and the corporations that dominate what we eat.

What has happened now is we are part of the phenomenon known as 'convenience'. Everybody wants everything yesterday and nobody wants to work for anything or provide for themselves. Towns and Cities awash with convenience stores on every street corner it seems, the 'fast food' generation or should I say the junk food generation. These corporations are more than happy to provide you with a cheap meal quickly so you don't have to prepare one yourself, you don't even have to walk into the restaurant or even get out of your car its so convenient. Yet the cost is more than just a few pounds, moreover your actual health. These places make sure to use the cheapest quality ingredients, often they are nothing more than chemicals! The 'food' is full of sugar and addictive substances to ensure that you keep on coming back for more time and again, and of course they make sure its cheap.

Same with health and doctors, people expect to spend their lives eating rubbish, drinking, smoking, and not exercising, yet maintain a good level of health? Then they expect that after years of abuse, popping a few pills given to them by the doctor who is probably on commission, is suddenly and magically going to cure all of your ailments. Of course the pill may cure a symptom but then another symptom will pop up, which is what western 'medicine' is all about, because you're never going to the root cause which is an actual lifestyle change. People don't want to do that, firstly it takes too long, and secondly it takes sacrifice. Much easier to just take a whole load of pills. Unfortunately Nature doesn't work that way, its simple 'cause and effect' if you have abused your body for years, it is going to take years of committed lifestyle change if you really want to be healthy. Ive done it myself, my health was rapidly going down the toilet about five years ago, my body was giving me all kinds of signals. Luckily I've never really trusted doctors and I understood it would take sacrifice, fast forward five years and I feel better and healthier than I did when I was 21 years old. Only through committed changes will the underlying issues heal themselves properly and more long lasting,

Mainstream medicine is like papering over the cracks, more and more pills for an array of symptoms. Its quite common to see people with almost a suitcase full of pills these days, yet ask them to change their diet or start exercising and they don't want to know. Many don't learn until the dam breaks and it gets so bad that they are forced to, and for many sometimes that moment comes too late. Again who wins out of this? Could it be big Pharma (interesting that the word 'harm' can be found within!) who supposedly have our best interests at heart? These companies are lying in bed with the food industry. Our society as a whole is extremely sick, cancer rates through the roof, a 50% chance of developing cancer now if you live in the UK! Dementia, alzeimers, heart disease yet nobody seems to be connecting the dots? People will argue that we are living longer, are we? A measly 70/80 years is supposed to be a good innings? Im convinced we can live much much longer, in fact there are many reports of people in ancient times living hundreds of years! We are not living longer, we are dying longer and there is a huge difference. People are getting sick in their late 30s early 40s nowadays and this cannot be right.

Where was all this cancer, diabetes etc as recent as 20 years ago? It was much rarer to hear of cancer, now there is not one person who has not either been affected themselves or has a relative who hasn't. Again we have become lazy, we have given our power and trust away to companies who provide food if you can even call it that. Absolutely loaded with chemicals, sugar, salt, msgs, and gmos, these things are foreign to the human body, the body only understands food that is natural. It can only take so much Frankenstein food before it starts to reject it and break down, which is when these sicknesses and diseases start, that also along with the stressful lives people lead. Not only does this effect our bodies but it effects our minds, it slows us down, makes us passive, withdrawn from life. I talk from personal experience of what my own diet used to be like, I used to consume all kinds of rubbish, and I started to suffer from bad digestive issues. As soon as I cut out the junk and switched to a plant based diet which is the most natural to the human body, my digestion improved, along with all my other issues, and it all went away almost overnight. That is not a coincidence, there is a direct correlation between diet and health, something the food industry and big pharma want to keep you in the dark about.

Like I say handing over our power has seen us being taken advantage of, we go to the doctors when we are sick who have only been trained from the manuals that advocate these drugs companies 'medicines' in many cases doctors are even on commission to push certain drugs. This can never be right, when health becomes a sales job you know we're in trouble. Chemotherapy and radiation which not only kills the bad cells in people but the good ones too, has an awful success rate, something like 98% failure rate, and those that do survive are left with horrendous issues afterwards and an average life span of just 15 years IF they survive. Blasting the human body with radiation doesn't even make logical sense yet doctors are commissioned to make sure people keep having this 'treatment'. This is so much worse when you consider the multiple natural cures that are being suppressed which is absolutely criminal. This is not about peoples health it is about money.

We have to come away from this idea that the food and medical industry have our best interests at heart, we need to take full control of our own health and what we are putting into our bodies, or at the very least demand that the food we are being sold is of a standard that it can be properly assimilated by the body. This situation gets worse unless we start boycotting what no longer serves us because it's a simple 'supply and demand' situation. The only thing these corporations understand is profit. Stop buying it and they will have to provide more of what we do want. On the positive side we are starting to see this happen more and more with organic and healthy products. Its encouraging to see people realizing and looking to adopt a more natural and fitness based lifestyle. The upturn of this is that we are starting to see an abundance of good wholesome, nutritious food on offer, and long may it continue.

We should be seriously asking questions as to why there are so many chemicals in our food in the first place, particularly salt and sugar which is actually more addictive than cocaine. It really is devastating to the human body when you research into it, and where do we see it most of all? Packed into food children love, sweets, biscuits, chocolate etc All presented in shiny, colorful packaging to catch their eyes whilst they are out shopping with mummy and daddy. They demand it and the parents supply without even really considering what is even in the product. Why are they always in these shiny packaging in the first place, and why do they make all this junk so cheap to buy? Its always on offer as soon as you walk through the entrance of a Tescos or a Wallmart the entrance is flooded with offers on junk? When was the last time you saw an avocado or a pear on offer or presented in a bright, eye catching package? A salad bowl in illuminous pink or purple with clown faces on it? Nobody thinks about that its too inconvenient, they might have to make changes to their lives. I cant wait to see the day where I don't drive past a billboard for McDonalds but see one for kale! This has to be one of the most evil companies on the Planet, luring kids in with their 'happy meals' and Ronald McDonald, yet absolutely loaded with sugar and chemicals. Have a look into how many chemicals are in chicken Mcnuggets its around the 50 mark! Of course this is early conditioning too so they grow up thinking this crap is normal and carry on buying it. Who's to blame though, the evil food companies providing and luring the children in or the parents who just give in to it all because they think that somehow this symbolizes love?

Back to convenience where you can radiate a microwave meal that will fill you up in minutes, yet that same convenience may well contribute you to getting a disease in years to come. Radiation CAUSES cancer yet we are radiating our food?! You couldn't make this up! Its all dirt cheap so as people struggle financially they literally have no option but to buy all this. Try putting together a decent salad with organic ingredients and you will be looking upwards of 15 pounds, yet buying a microwave Shepherds pie and you can probably get one for just a pound! No just keep on consuming crap so that you are too tired , lethargic, and dumbed down to do anything about the longer working hours, mass corruption, and rife paedophillia that is infesting our society. Again this is not an accident folks! Take GMOS which if you live in America you literally cannot get away from. Not only is the food genetically modified but the food genetically modifies us! It actually changes our DNA and dumbs us down. They have also done experiments on rats where it makes the third generation sterile, and also causes cancerous tumors. But keep on shopping folks, all is well nothing to see here. As long as its quick, easy, and convenient then it doesn't really matter.

Take responsibility for what you're putting in your body, and that of your children, stop believing that these industries love and care for you, they care only about profit and keeping us sick, and stupid. If we all make better choices these companies will cease to exist. It might take a little more effort, cost, and preparation but what price can you put on your health? Lets move away from convenience and more into patience. Any solution has to start with our physical health, our temples, that is where self love starts, if you are eating junk, not exercising etc do you really love yourself? Our bodies are literally made up of what we eat and every 7 years our cells regenerate and are made out of what we consume. So it can be expected that filling ourselves up on low vibrational, unhealthy food designed to keep us stupid will make a population of low vibrational stupid people.

This also works mentally too in terms of what you are putting into your mind, If you put junk in, junk will be the output. If people spend time watching pointless mind dumbing TV soaps, reality shows, and do no work on the self, read books, or seek knowledge then again the outward manifestation of the general populace is going to be pretty dumbed down and stupid. It will be unthinking, unknowledgeable, and unquestioning, which if we are being honest with ourselves is what we have right now. TV watchers that just believe everything the black box in their living room tells them, stuffing their face with junk. Look at the way people who seek knowledge, read, expand their minds, or basically just like to do more productive things with their time are perceived in society. Geeks, nerds, loners, the list goes on. We live in a society where knowledge is 'uncool' and being dumb is celebrated. Look at the new idols people worship these days, the likes of Paris Hilton and Kim Kardashian. These so called 'celebrities' are the epitome of the current mindset of humanity. Literal know nothings, or at least that is what they show to the World anyway who promote that being stupid is somehow 'cute' idolised by billions.

What they are also great at promoting of course is getting people looking outside of themselves for happiness which of course will never happen. Its all about how you look with these people, what label is on your shoes and bags, constantly banging the drum on their appearance, telling others how they should look, and if they don't well that's just too bad and somehow they have failed at life. Not literally of course, but this is the general undertone. We are now living in the age of the 'selfie' yet no knowledge of self. Some people will go through their entire lives without having any understanding of the working of their own minds, yet I guarantee you they will know the top three eyeliners to wear, or what branded shirt looks best with jeans and trainers.

What happened to the thirst for knowledge in society? When did we lose it and why? This is such a magical, interesting World we live in, one could live a million lifetimes and still not scratch the surface when it comes to gaining all the knowledge there is to gain. So why are people so comfortable with firstly being told by a black box what is real and what is not, but secondly quite content that that just five channels will tell them all they ever need to know in life? People don't read anymore, they're not interested in it because it takes up too much time and effort, it goes back to this convenience culture again. They might have to think, imagine, discern information, you know all those things we are SUPPOSED to be doing. Its much easier to just slouch back in the armchair with a burger and a coke and let the black box tell you everything you need to know.

Yet the cycle continues as children are thrust in front of the television as soon as they are out of their cots, conditioned from birth to be conditioned by the TV. So it really shouldn't come as a surprise that we are a World of TV watchers. Imagine living your entire life, getting your lowdown on everything that happens on the Planet from this black box in the corner of your room?! Yet people do it, and it only benefits those in power who control those 5 channels. They can propagate anything knowing people will believe it as gospel, and of course the TV would never lie to us would it?!

If people only knew or did the research into what the TV does to the mind then they may just think twice about watching it. As human beings we operate on varying brain wave functions which are alpha, beta, delta, and theta. Our normal resting state is that of beta, this is where we are just going about our daily lives with a certain level of awareness and alertness. This is important when we talk of both the conscious and subconscious minds. Imagine the conscious mind as like the firewall for your computer, filtering information as it comes in and protecting your PC from anything negative or viruses. Your subconscious mind literally cannot think for itself, however if anything gets through and reaches the subconscious it will just react on that information, whatever gets through becomes ideas, viewpoints, and opinions about the World, it becomes our very belief systems. So the conscious mind is extremely important in filtering what comes through to the subconscious. For example you are reading this book now so your mind is operating at a normal resting 'beta' rate, and your conscious mind is taking in all the information and discerning whether or not it is true, it then either allows(or doesn't) the information through to your subconscious. Like I said if this is allowed through to the subconscious this will play out in the real World as new opinions, ideas etc. Now what happens when you watch TV is that the actual frequency the television omits literally changes your brainwave pattern from beta to a much more suggestible alpha state. This is almost like a hypnotic trance state, where your conscious mind (firewall) has now been sufficiently relaxed and lowered, almost like being 'off guard' which now totally exposes the subconscious mind to the information coming from the television. This is why when you look at people when they are watching TV they actually look like they are in a trance, because mentally that is what is going on, zombified with mouth slightly aghast. Then what happens when they have you in that hypnotic state? That's right they hit you with all the advertisements, subliminals, and propaganda, telling you that you need to buy shit you don't need, telling you what junk food to eat, how to act, look, and think. You are quite literally being programmed, and that's why after all they are called TV PROGRAMS! Telling a lie to your vision repeating the same thing day after day, week after week, year after year. "You must fear terrorists' "you must hate Muslims' 'You must eat McDonalds' Your subconscious mind is being bombarded with bullshit when your guard is down. Billions of pounds a year are made from companies advertising on TV, and God only knows how many billions across the Planet getting hypnotized to beLIEve (there it is again in the very word) State propaganda to gain support for yet another bombing campaign in some far away oil rich land.

Repetition is also another form of hypnosis which is why you hear politicians repeat the same things over and over again. "Freedom' this and 'freedom' that or 'change, change, change' this is drummed into the minds of the masses to the point where they start believing whatever is being said by whatever puppet politician is saying standing in front of them. Im sorry but if we are so 'free' then why do they need to keep repeating it so often? It should be self evident!

The other aspect of watching TV we need to be aware of are the subliminals, these can be in the form of symbols, siduals, pictures, or innuendoes that are flashed quickly within programs and advertisements that completely bypass the conscious mind. When a message is hidden or happens so quickly then it reaches straight through to the subconscious mind, again having a long lasting effect on our belief systems, behavior, and opinions about the World. These are extremely prominent in childrens programs and unfortunately many times of a hyper sexualized Nature. Its shocking to hear but the minds of our young are being corrupted at a very young age. Research sexual subliminals in Disney films, it's beyond shocking. Just look at the idols for the young these days people like Miley Cyrus, and Rhianna who even released a song called S&M! This is going on folks right in front of our faces, a continuous sexualisation of society and in particular targeting the young. It's all there researchable if you care to know, be very careful what your child is sitting watching.

A child's mind up until the age of 8 is like a sponge, in terms of brainwave patterns children are operating at a theta wave state making them absolutely wide open and susceptible to everything around them and what they see and hear. This is why children are such quick learners because they soak things up so quickly. Most parents on some level know this so it begs the question why are we allowing them to sit in front of something for hours that we have no control over what comes out. We just assume its all good information that isn't harmful or detrimental to the child. Parents trust the information and programs on TV are just harmless and fun. This is not the case and that black box is shaping their belief systems for years to come. Parents are no longer in control of what the children grow up thinking, the TV is.

It gets even more interesting when you start learning about color frequencies which also have a profound effect on human consciousness and the mind. If you take the color green for example this represents balance, Nature is abundant in the color green because it is balanced itself. So we see green used a lot in advertising with big oil companies such as BP using this frequency. To the product being sold this color makes it a lot more attractive to the consumer. What is very interesting are the colors blue and red which are extremely prominent in news broadcasts. Red to the subconscious mind literally means 'stop pay attention' (think of red on traffic lights) red gets your attention, then comes the blue which opens up the subconscious mind and makes it much more suggestible, or put another way easier to manipulate. Think of all the major news companies BBC, CNN, Fox News, and even Alex Jones and Infowars (who I do not trust) these programs are smothered in blues and reds. This is not by coincidence it's by design because they know these colors have a profound effect on the human psyche. Let's get one thing straight TV was never created for your entertainment, it was created to manipulate minds and to shape and mold entire societies to suit the people running the show.

Most words, phrases, fashions, and trends at some point were rooted in TV and advertising. People need to understand that their minds are programmable and they need to be vidgilent of what software they are allowing to be downloaded into themselves and their family members. Think about it where would all the hate for immigrants or Muslims come from if it wasn't for the TV? They have managed to sell entire Wars to people, massacring millions along the way based on continuous propaganda spouted from that stupid box that everyone worships like a God. It is the focal point or the center piece in everyones home these days, where whole families sit and hang off of its every word, and unless a story or angle comes from there then it cannot be true! Its madness. We have 'living rooms' where peoples minds are dying!

When you look at these soaps or programs they are shocking. Many soaps are full of violence, alcoholism, siblings fighting against each other, affairs etc I mean is it really any wonder we live in a society plagued by those very behavior patterns when they are being aired 24/7? Talk shows where guests have physical fights on stage with each other spilling their most private issues to the Nation, are we really that desperate to be entertained that we need to resort to watching other peoples car crash lives? What does that say about our own lives when we even have the time to do that? Most of these people need love, help, and support. They are being exploited for a weird, sick, and twisted need for shallow and mindless entertainment. Do these programs make folk feel better about their own sad lives? Im sure there is something in that, air people that have completely lost their way in the most disturbing of ways and the rest of the population will feel better about their own existence.

There is now even a TV program in the UK called 'Gogglebox' which actually involves watching people on TV watching people on TV! This is the trash people are filling their minds with on a daily basis, a dumb generation that loves being dumb and wants to get even dumber, sitting there eating food that is dumbing them down at the same time. What an absolute waste of a human life. Where is the desire to learn about your own existence, mind, spirituality? I don't get how people would prefer to sit there and watch a depressing program about an A&E ward in a hospital where some guy is having a triple by pass operation! Each to their own of course, but my purpose is to point out why society is in such an utter state and why we are losing our rights and freedoms by the day, and we need to look no further than this weapon of mass distraction. It's the same with the newspapers, pointless stories in the main that mean nothing, filled with useless crap about celebrity gossip, who is sleeping with who, and who kicked the football in the goal the most times the previous day, nothing that effects our everyday lives.

TV stations and newspapers are all owned by the same people, the 1% who like to keep us living in ignorance and servitude to them. There are something like 1500 newspapers, 1100 magazines, 9000 radio stations, 1500 TV stations, and 2400 publishers all owned by just the same 6 companies, does that sound like a free unbiased media to you? The implications for freedom of information are huge. Who are these people and what is their agenda? They are all spewing out more or less the same information on a daily basis with perhaps a slightly different spin. A report by either CNN and BBC for example wont be too far apart in what they report and the underlying storyline. As soon as a bomb has gone off we are told within minutes almost who is responsible (normally a Muslim who has kindly left their passport or ID card at the scene, and their name is Mohammed). CNN, Fox, The Sun newspaper, Daily Mail, New York Times all will report the same set of circumstances generally. I would say that this is an extreme example but its not.

In the year of 2016 there have been more so called 'terrorist attacks' than ever before, I literally lost count in June and they all follow the same rhetoric. Bomb goes off or lone gunman, we then get told who is responsible, passport/ID card is found, if it's a Muslim or someone from ISIS (a fabrication of the west) we then need to go and drop more bombs to stop the terrorists. If it's a lone gun man (always in America because that's one of the only Countries left who are legally allowed to own guns which prevents the government from fully taking over) then we get told there needs to be a ban on guns or tighter gun laws. This process is actually a technique in which governments further their own agendas covertly it is called the 'hegelian dialectic' or as researchers such as David Icke have coined it 'problem, reaction, solution'.

This technique has been used for hundreds of years as a way for governments to further their plans but in a covert way in which the masses won't be suspicious. It is a way in which they can sway public opinion to suit because of an incident lets say a bomb or attack. This is an incident that is either pre-ordained with full knowledge of the government, or is actually government sponsored terrorism that they are fully aware of. Again 9/11 is probably the best example to use for this as I have already mentioned there are holes all over the official version of event, in fact it is so badly matched up when you compare the so called 'evidence' eye witness statements, and inconsistencies that it almost beggars belief that anyone with a half operating brain would believe this version. What 9/11 was REALLY about was going back into Iraq to finish the job of George Bush senior, it was about creating a continuous 'War on terror' which will never have a time limit because after all how do you know when you have all the terror? This suits the people that love War and death, and of course all the weapons manufacterers. It was about the development of not just a totalitarian State in America but a totalitarian World where we are all constantly monitored, surveilled and spyed on. A World where because of that one single event our rights and freedoms have been eroded to such an extent we are almost walking around in Orwells 1984. Yes there are people who want the World like this and they want the World enslaved, and 9/11 was a huge stepping stone for them to be able to do that. The world changed forever after that event, again I am not going to go into the ins and outs of it all here only to encourage people to research with an open mind.

This isn't the only incident people need to research though, we need to critically discern everything we are being told after these events and ask ourselves who benefits? Will these events lead to more bombing attacks from the west? Tighter gun laws? In the alternative media community these pre-ordained or even fabricated attacks are known as 'false flags'. Unbelievably it has been discovered that 'crisis actors' have been used in these events. That's not to say that people don't die, but there is certainly an extremely high level of deception going on in most cases.

Notice many times there is no mobile phone footage, in an era where everything is being filmed. These same actors seem to pop up in numerous different incidents, there was the case of one girl being part of the Boston bombing and then she popped up again in the Paris shooting! This is not unusual there is much more going on than what you see on the face of it, certainly on the mainstream media news channels. I would highly recommend people look into the work of Ole Dammegard when it comes to false flag events. Huge amount of research has gone into his work, and his ability to debunk the official versions is basically second to none.

I could literally write another book going into the details and the sheer absurdities in some of the fairy tales we are told but my purpose here is just to get you the reader to question, first in your own mind in the hope you will then take it upon yourself to go and do the necessary research. So called 'journalism' today is dead, news reporters are told WHAT they can write and speak about, they are not going out and digging for information and getting both sides of the story, again just like the other order followers for the system they will only do what they are told because a pay cheque depends on them doing so. I was once on holiday in Thailand where I met some reporters for the Daily Mirror they were a bit drunk and so I asked them do they just report what they are told? They looked at me and laughed and said yes of course they do! I wasn't shocked but I wanted to hold them to account over this and proceeded to tell them that they are doing the Nation a huge disservice and that I thought it was terrible they found it so funny that they were potentially lying to all these people on a daily basis. Well as you can imagine they got really angry with me, started swearing and stormed off! This is what we are dealing with in the mainstream folks. Now Im not saying everything on the internet is true either but at least there is a wide variety of sources to discern from and not just one official version.

The reason why this technique is so potent in directing a society is because it plays on human emotions and fear, so broken down it works like this. Just say you want to introduce a fully locked down surveillance State, and you want not only a War with Iraq but a continuous War that will last decades and decades, you cant just go ahead and start that War without reason, you need an excuse otherwise the people will say 'hey you cannot do that' so you create the problem i.e 9/11. So then once you have created this horrific event clearly the population in their state of horror and fear are going to look at the government for 'protection' (oh the irony) as if to say 'what are you going to do to stop this?' Then you offer the solution (which was the target all along) to go and bomb the Middle East and introduce more surveillance. Its so simple yet devastating and its being used on us all the time over and over again and we desperately need to wise up to this.

For as long as people think that these governments care about us and wouldn't do that to their own people we will remain in the dark. The psychopaths have no problems bombing small children, so why do you think they would have a problem killing their own? They don't think like us because they're not like us literally. Ask yourself if you were in a room with 10 other people and you asked them if they wanted War what would they say? Of course they wouldn't want War. Yet we are always at War?

Continuing along the lines of TV, games, and distractions can there be a bigger one than sport? Now it may seem to the reader that I am knocking everything that is enjoyable in the World but its really not the case, Im simply trying to get to the root cause as to WHY the few have so much and everyone else is feeding off the scraps and sport plays a massive role in that. Don't get me wrong I actually love sport and play football regularly, I also watch quite a few games and follow my local team Southend United for my sins, I swim, run, and in general sport has been a massive release and comfort for me down the years, especially when dealing with the ills of the World. The difference is that I see it for what it is, Im not totally consumed by it as many find themselves (although I admit I did used to be). Walk into any office or go into any bar or pub chances are the discussions will evolve around football. Who are United going to sign for a ridiculous fee next? What will Arsenal's formation against Tottenham at the weekend be?

People plan their whole weekends around games, and the incidents from those games being talked about over and over again for weeks, newspapers full of transfer gossip. It's just another Religion and for many folk they go to the alter and pray to their individual Gods at 3pm on a Saturday afternoon! The sheer amount of passion displayed from football fans in relation to their team is quite staggering, they will sing chant, argue, and even fight over the shirt and bragging rights. All this hysteria for kicking a ball in between two posts. I know people that if Arsenal lose at the weekend then their whole weekend will be ruined! Like I say don't get me wrong I like it when my team wins but I'm not going to hang myself over it. It's not life or death to me its just a game, just like all the other sports people are obsessed with.

Why such a problem with this you ask? Well it's the sheer disparity of care between a simple game and issues that REALLY matter in this World. Where is the same passion for the 100,000 children that went missing in the UK last year, the illegal Wars going on all the time, or the increasing amount of chemicals in our food, water, and air supplies? You know those things that effect our EVERYDAY lives and the lives of future generations if we do nothing about it. Yet there is more uproar for a bad offside decision than there is another politician being caught involved in a child abuse case? This cannot be right. If people only used the same passion displayed in football matches and used that passion to directly try and effect World issues then things would change on a dime. This is simple 'bread and circuses' by the ruling class, again just another manipulation that has been going on centuries since people used to gather at the Colluseum in Roman times. Distractions everywhere it's the same all over the World although the sport may differ slightly so if you're in the States it's American football, baseball, basketball etc, as long as there is the big game at the weekend that the masses can get hyped up about particularly the men.

Historically and traditionally the men have always been seen as the 'protectors' in society. The woman knits the family together with her love and nurture and the men provides and protects, these are just facts of life and how the masculine and feminine energy are supposed to function, dovetailing each other and intertwining these sacred qualities. This is despite the huge transgender agenda being pushed out right now from the media which is designed to confuse the sexes and bastardise these roles to make the population easier to control. But that's another subject all together. The male in society can almost be depicted as the warrior archetype in that if there is a threat to his family or the community at large then he will stand up for them and if necessary fight. I ask myself where are the warriors in todays society when the women and children need them now? In a nut shell they are in a bar or down the pub watching the game, getting all worked up about some high tackle or an own goal somebody scored.

Men today I have to say are an embarrassment, not all men of course there are a few who are taking a stand against injustice and the constant erosion of our freedoms, but where are all the others? It is their offspring that is in danger and they couldn't care less, dumbed down, drunk, and down the pub. No guts, no courage, and most of all no care or purpose. I wonder what some of the ancient ancestors would think of men these days? These men used to give their lives for their societies. Let's be honest with ourselves men have turned into cowards, scared of what their wife, friends, sister, or government will say if they dare speak out or do anything, the complete destruction of their masculine core. I know many men who are aware of certain truths who like I have said, choose to do nothing, to watch and stand on the sidelines as their children's World is being destroyed in front of their faces. It's nothing more than a disgrace.

I'm not just singling out men here but really men should be leading the way, not only protecting the women and children but the very blueprint of the sacred feminine energy. Men have to be the cradle for the feminine to feel safe to express itself which I have said already is about love, care, creativity, and nurture. The truth is most women don't feel safe these days. Men are not showing up in the World how they are supposed to so what they do then is hand over more of their power to governments and the cycle perpetuates. These feminine qualities are almost dead in the World, hanging by a literal thread. How will these the World ever heal without this nurturing energy if its cannot express itself or doesn't feel safe to do so?

The distractions are most certainly there for women too, shopping seems to be the number one past time to waste their lives on. Of course shopping hones in on how important it is to look good and to keep looking at your outer shell for happiness rather than going within. Its all about how you look. In a way I feel sorry for women as there is so much pressure on them to look beautiful which of course starts from a young age with the 'princess programming' they get from Disney films etc with their near faultless characters. Then as they grow up its just a constant bombardment of advertisements on the TV and in newspapers and magazines telling women how they are somehow lacking in one department or another, whether that be their lips, hair or breasts its all about making them not feel good enough. Most of the adverts are airbrushed too so it would be almost impossible to look that good anyway! Women are never encouraged to go within, seek knowledge, spirituality, or read books, its only about looks. Is it any wonder so many women feel so insecure with this daily assault on their psyches?

So of course the natural response is to go out and buy all these clothes, garments, and botox that will apparently lead to eternal happiness. Even men are being targeted now as they are being turned more feminine anyway. Men pouting like women, I think there are more men in sun bed shops now than women! So we have become a population filled with insecurities about our outward appearance all the time. Im not saying that there is anything wrong wiith wanting to look nice not at all, but its this obsessive behavior of the 'selfie generation'. These magazines and articles are just not true, they want you to feel shit about yourself so you go out and buy their products. Throw those magazines where they belong, in the bin! We are ALL already beautiful its just another way in which we have lost our power.

## THE HIDDEN HANDS

The people pulling the strings in this World are quite different in their psyches compared to the rest of us. Now I could go metaphysical here as there are other interpretations of what is in control, but at this stage its easier to explain the mentality, and here I am talking about psychopathy. A psychopath is someone who doesn't have the empathy gene, it just wants complete power and dominance no matter what. They don't care what they do to get what they want they will just do it anyway. It is estimated that around 2-4% of the Worlds population are what we call 'primary psychopaths' this condition is something people are born like, it cannot be cured, these people because of their Nature of getting what they want however they want tend to find themselves in leadership positions say in governments, the banking industry, or heads of large corporations. There is a literal disconnect in their brain which prevents them from feeling compassion. We are literally co-existing with another species folks that's the harsh reality of it. Yet it explains so much, it explains why there is so much evil in this World because most humans are not evil, most humans want peace, love, happiness, and connection. Yet we have the opposite, and the reason is because these people are not like us. They are expert deceivers and you probably wouldn't even know on the surface that they are one.

They can be charming, witty, intelligent, and say all the right things (just look at politicians!) yet under the surface we are dealing with another animal. They are the perfect actors and actresses masquerading as people that care about us and want the best for us, yet in reality they are predators.

Unfortunately what they have done is turned many of us into their image with what we call 'secondary psychopathy'. This other version is where people are not born psychopaths but are trained to think like psychopaths I mean just think about the Military and Police trained to be cold, calculated, and heartless. Literally rubbing out the empathy gene to the point where they would kill their fellow human being. These are obviously the extreme versions of the secondary psychopaths existing within the human race, personally I think that a lot of humanity is suffering with a milder version of secondary psychopathy, I mean look how we treat each other in general, we are hardly a populace of empathetic and compassionate people these days. Most of us are out for ourselves and couldn't really care less how we get what we want, and these are exactly the same traits of the psychopath albeit to a milder form. Understanding these dynamics exist is the first step to healing them, being aware we can shield ourselves and shield our loved ones. We do after all outnumber these people hugely, and if we can stop doing their work for them and realise they are turning us into them them then that is a huge step in stopping the train in its tracks. What other choice do we have after all? They rely on keeping this in the shadows, they thrive because people don't know what we are dealing with here. We are giving them the power that they crave all the time. I have even wondered that could they be here in existence to even force humanity to evolve, after all the Universe will keep giving us the same problems until we learn our lessons. Maybe just maybe if we stood up to bullies and started to stand on our own two feet they would have very little influence on our lives. Stop fighting their wars, down tools so to speak when it comes to them making immoral laws and rules up. Don't play their game.

We also cannot judge these monsters by our own moral compass, this is often the case when you mention events such as 9/11 being an inside job. People immediately get upset and will say statements like 'surely they wouldn't do that?' of course its horrifying to even consider that these God like figures in government who supposedly are there to babysit us would be involved in such a crime, yet they take this view because they are coming at it from an angle like these people are just like us. They're not, they dont have an ounce of empathy for the general public, we are just pawns to be used to dominate and control. The only use we have to them is to siphon us of our hard work, resources, and on a deeper level our energy. To realise those in power are basically like another species is the first step to understanding why the World is as it is. Why there is constant turmoil, Wars, and struggle. Its designed this way, and actually they quite enjoy standing back and watching the suffering, thats what a psychopath is.

Any long lasting solutions will only come when we all start to heal ourselves, the realisation that they have manipulated our minds to be like them is the first step towards changing things around. Human beings are not like this in our inherent Nature, we do have empathy, care, courage, and in our true state are natural healers, and once we rediscover the very parts of ourselves that they dont want us to realise then we will be able to make positive changes. The very reason that people don't care about the state of the World is because, like I have mentioned, at some level they don't care about themselves. We can only ever find true happiness within, no external influences or even other relationships will fill the void unless we fill it ourselves. No material goods, make up, or jewellery will replace what your soul really wants and that is to realise its already perfect. A loving Planet will only manifest when we love ourselves and all this bullshit is just another way that they can keep our eye of the prize. We are what we have been waiting for literally.

Unlike primary psychopathy, which as I say you are born with, secondary psychopathy can be healed. For example we are seeing more and more police brutality going on by the day, my Facebook feed is often filled with aggressive police officers beating or tasing folk for the smallest of things, people that are oftentimes out to demonstrate for a good cause, and the treatment in many cases is unbelieveable. No sane person with a stable mind would behave in such a way, in my view you have to be mentally ill to want to do that for a 'living'. There is something within the pysche that is not functioning, and as far as I can see it is the disconnect from emapthy, or in other words psychopathy. Same with bailiffs, military, or any of those other roles in society that we have accepted as the norm, if you are willing to inflict such barbaric treatment on your fellow man or woman then you are not all the ticket.

It's like this because the empathy is beaten out of them through rigorous training regimes. The military are trained to think that general civilians are basically the enemy. Look at what they go through, their peers bellowing and repeating different mind altering ideaologies in their faces waiting for the obligatory 'YES SIR' responses. Drummed into their heads that killing innocent people is just 'collateral damage' that is certainly NOT the viewpoint of an empathetic being, that is the view of a psychopath. So we see how programmable we are again, many of these servants of the State initially (through brainwashing) may have good intentions and believe they are serving the general pubic (oh the irony) when in actual fact they go to get their humanity beaten out of them to be another cog in the system of psychopathy. My point is that they can give us their minds through indoctrination, repetition, and training.

We also have to realise like I have said that psychopaths are extremely cunning and smart, how else do they get to be the heads of large corporations or governments. They are master manipulators, the ultimate shmoozers, and absolutely brilliant actors. This is why they have been able to get away with it for so long because on the surface if you met a psychopath you probably wouldnt even realise it. Just watch how politicians can lie on TV in front of millions of people yet at the same time ensnare peoples minds. Devious and ruthless, and would have no issue saying or doing whatever is necessary to see them to rise to the top. Their minds are wired to want more, more power, control, money, or whatever they may be looking to feast on. Their very existenece is that of a parasite, it wants to feed and feed until it ceases to exist. This parasite if we are not careful is on its way to devouring humanity whole if we dont wake up soon. Its not the most pleasant of realisations I appreciate that, yet the day that was explained to me the whole World made sense.

# THE CONFUSION OF THE SEXES

As you delve deeper down the rabbit hole it is quite clear that there is a blatant war going on both the sexes to confuse and create division, to muddy the lines so as genders we don't even know what our roles are in the World anymore, there is as I have discussed, an inversion on both the masculine and feminine energies, with men acting more like women and visa versa. Men have lost their balls when it comes to issues at hand, but how has this come to pass? The manipulation on not only the mind but on the physical bodies of men is extremely disturbing when you shine a light on the subject. For example the female hormone oestrogen is rampant in our food and water supplies, particularly bottled water, the question is WHY would this need to be added at all?? Oestrogen lowers the testosterone levels in men and makes them more passive and lets be honest, literally more feminine. This isn't just affecting children and grown men either, studies have shown that a pregnant woman could be carrying a baby boy and if she is ingesting a lot of bisphenol A (an oestrogenic endocrine disruptor) the sex related genes can be switched on and off, in effect possibly causing the male baby to develop a female brain!

I want to make it clear at this point I have no problem with gay or transgender people, this isn't about that and its certainly not an attack on them, there has always been a percentage of these people and that's their choice, what I am talking about is an all out assault to take the masculine energy out of society. Where else do we see oestrogen in abundance? You guessed it in alcohol, meat, and dairy, so it's bad news for men sitting down the pub with their mates eating steak! Not only is it in the steak its in your beer too! If it wasn't so tragic it would be funny, all the guys being all 'blokey' down the pub consuming things that are making them more feminine!

It's not just in the food though just look at the constant garbage on the TV, just the fashion shows men wearing dresses etc Its all being completely normalized and propagated through media outlets, drip feeding it into our minds. The media is consistently talking about 'what does it actually mean to be a man?' or 'What constitutes being a woman?' I read somewhere that in a school there was a tick box for men, woman, and neither! Just the other week I was on the BBC website where it asked me to fill in a form where the gender options were man, woman, or other!Where has all this sprung from all of a sudden? In nightclubs now there are mixed toilets, its all going on both overtly and covertly, and it explains why, at least in part men don't act like men anymore, because physically and mentally they are being changed, chemically and through mind control.

The divine feminine energy is also under heavy assault, that energy of care, creativity, and nurture. The very energy that is needed to change the World. If people care about things then it's a lot harder for others to dominate. Instead females are increasingly being turned aggressive and competitive, they are completely operating from their masculine in this capitalist society. Instead of being in their innate feminine qualities they are being turned into ruthless 'winner takes all' robots. This has not come to pass by coincidence I might add, it came with the rise of feminism and the feminist movement in general, which if you do the research was actually created and funded by the Rockerfeller foundation because they wanted to tax the other half of the population which they were missing out on. It was also to start the break up of the family unit so the children would be spending more time with the State at school and less time with the parents. Obviously I am not saying here that women should not have rights, not at all. The way women have been viewed as less than men, bastardised, and abused throughout history is one of the biggest crimes ever committed by humanity. Im saying this was done to create a new type of female, to take women further away from their inherent qualities that they are born with.

Now we have a situation where both parents are out at work all the time partly because they cannot afford not to be either. The traditional roles have been perverted with women also encouraged to be promiscuous, as I say the lines have been muddied. The World desperately needs women to regain their femininity, their love, and their care. The Planet is stuck in an overtly male dominated, left brained, mindset and there has to be balance. The male energy should be there to protect the female energy, soon we will be living in a World where neither energy exists. No care or love, and nobody to protect.

Again I'm not suggesting women stay at home all day and don't have careers but anyone with half a brain who has observed the societal decline in recent decades should be able to see where I am coming from. Men used to stand up and protect and women used to hold things together like glue with their love and care.

Could this also be why so many relationships fail? In one sense I feel it's because of the 'convenience' factor again? When things go wrong people quickly look for somebody else to feel the void in their own hearts, normally this is down to a lack of self love, but I also think that a huge part of it is that men and women are acting so abnormally these days due to these new constructs that turns the other partner off? I hear a lot from women these days who complain that men no longer act like men. But at the same time I know men, and Ive felt this myself, that women no longer act like women either. Men are indoctrinated by all these movies where the guy is all soppy and needy and the women eventually falls in love. Im not saying that there is no need for a feminine side in men Im just explaining the constant bombardment of how these energies are being manipulated on different levels.

The World is getting crazier now trangender, trans-neutral now where a person doesn't identify with neither a man or a woman, I have even seen people coming out and saying they now identify with certain animals! I mean if this is the case we can just be anything we want right? I can now wake up in the morning and say that I'm a dolphin! Sorry not sorry, if you're born with a penis you're a male, if you're born with a vagina you're a female. Try broaching this subject though and you are classed as a bigot, or a homophobe! I am not saying that there isn't a small percentage of tortured souls who are born and genuinely feel that they may have been born into the wrong body, there has always been a tiny percentage of these people. What I am talking about is this, what has now become at least, a fashion trend where everyone wants to be something that they're not. This 'movement' if that's what you want to call it seems to be a place where damaged people can go and instead of genuinely trying to heal themselves and whatever issues they have, they run to this because it gives them a sense of belonging, a way to channel their anger at the World and stay in victim consciousness, It's nothing more than a trend pedalled out by those that understand the energy dynamics of both males and females and want to stamp it out. A confused population without these energies at the core is a walkover, the lines are being muddied and they're being muddied on purpose.

Unfortunately another unpopular viewpoint which needs to be said is the fact that transgender and now paedophillia are being lumped into the gay rights movement. The reason for this is because lumping paedophillia in within the gay rights, somehow (in their eyes anyways) seems to water it all down. Just look at the recent case with the actor Kevin Spacey for example, accused of child abuse and what was his response? His stance was that it was because he was gay! Like that suddenly makes everything all right! His is the most high profile case of this merging with gay rights to date, however anyone with an eagle eye would have noticed as the years have passed how it has cleverly been introduced now as one of the same thing. Again I dont have any axe to grind with gay people I'm just saying what I see, and the truth is not enough people are talking about this. Paedophillia is absolutely rife in this World with its tentacles in the highest echelons of society including government, Hollywood, and beyond. What better way to water it down at a time where all this is coming to the surface. Look out for more of this in years to come, and understand the very subtle mind maniplation going on.

# What's your poison?

The role of alcohol in society cannot be understated enough, it's extremely detrimental to our hormonal balance but it goes so much deeper than that. Now before I start I have to say I used to drink, I used to drink quite a bit back in the day, its just what you do right? Work all week then get hammered at the weekend. I couldn't tell you the number of times I went out and got pissed with my mates, all that money spent to feel like crap for three days afterwards! Thankfully Ive seen the light with it and maybe occasionally I might have a glass of red wine or a beer but even that is extremely rare these days.

This drinking culture we have is destructive beyond belief not just on a personal level in wrecking relationships, causing violence, and even in some cases early death through disease etc. But on a societal level it costing the taxpayer millions of pounds a year. Hospitals overburdened with patients at weekends and bank holidays, it generally causes havoc and destruction. You would imagine something like alcohol, looking at things on a surface level like that, would be illegal right? But its not so why is that?

Firstly when people get drunk they escape their own reality, the very root cause as to why they do it, they may argue like I once did, that it is 'fun' but surely you can have fun without literally poisoning yourself? They drink often to escape their 9-5 weekly cycle to forget for a few hours that they are slaves to a system that has stolen their freedom and couldn't care less about them. To paper over the cracks of their own discontentment and unhappiness instead of facing their issues head on. It is understandable to a degree as to why people do this, but it is just based in avoidance and does nothing to move either the person or society further forward. Of course people drink for all kinds of reasons to try and escape guilt, abuse, unworthiness but alcohol only serves to make these issues worse in the long run.

I'm only focusing on human freedom here in that this poison is given to us so we are too dumbed down, out of our faces, or depressed and hungover to rise up and and change anything in this World. Everyone is grinding during the week and then pissed up at the weekend watching the game or something. Like I say Ive done it myself, it makes you feel truly awful afterwards. Being completely honest the biggest mistakes I have made in my own life have been when I have been drunk, I couldn't have cared less about Worldly issues or the environment when I was getting drunk every weekend.

The health issues caused by alcohol are there for all to see and of course the main one is the destruction of the liver, one of the most important organs in the body to maintain good health. It helps to purify and detoxify the body of harmful toxins and substances. A fully functioning liver is essential to human health. Alcohol is also a thief of nutrients, people diets in general are already very poor with little to no nutrition, and whatever nutrition they are getting then gets obliterated by alcohol. Clearly drinking makes us feel worse afterwards as the body recovers from being literally poisoned (theres a lot of truth in that question whats your poison?!). For days this can linger, hardly something that makes a person want to go out and do anything positive in the World.

Alcohol is the worst drug out there, certainly worse than most other narcotics and certainly 100% more harmful than cannabis! How many incidents of violence or vandalism are based around somebody who was smoking a joint in their living room? How much damage to property? How many people end up in A&E after getting high? Generally the worst thing that can happen to pot smokers is that they may get a little paranoid or get the munchies and pig out on a load of junk food! Far far less destructive yet one is legal and the other is not? I'm not advocating cannabis either, there are negative side effects if you smoke it all the time, it can make people unmotivated and lazy, but comparing the two is like chalk and cheese in terms of the destruction of society. Just on the subject of cannabis the very notion of BANNING a plant in the first place is absolutely hilarious, like Nature could ever be banned or restricted by man! Just more BS we blindly accept as a society. People are destroying themselves and their lives getting wasted, and that suits the government just fine because whilst we are destroying ourselves we are not destroying the system that puts us in such a mindset whereby we need alcohol to actually escape our reality.

Look at the extent alcohol is advertised and glorified! TV adverts, football shirt sponsors where children watch their favorite players running around with Calsberg or Carling emblazed across their shirts and so are conditioned from an early age so the cycle continues. Its even promoted in the Olympic games (surely such an event should be promoting things that are good for health?). Lets get this straight alcohol is a HARD drug and should be viewed as such, lets start calling things as they are, a chemical induced drug that dumbs down the population and destroys their mind, bodies, and spirits (again is it just a coincidence that they are called 'spirits' either!)

TV is a drug, sugar is a drug, all these things we have been told to accept and embrace that we have accepted as normal are stealing and ruining our futures and those of generations to come. Yet try being the only one not drinking in any kind of social engagement and people look at you like you are an absolute freak of Nature! People cannot fathom that, God forbid, you might not want to poison yourself! They also just can't seem to have a good time without it, its become an addiction for many, a bad habit that they can't, or don't even want to break. It's a huge issue again that holds us back as a species and prevents us from becoming the best version of ourselves.

I wonder how many more lives need to be wrecked before the penny actually drops that this stuff needs to go. Certainly if we are serious about moving forward as a species then it must go. I pretty much live by the rule these days that if something was actually good for us then they wouldn't let us have it, and anything that is heavily advertised needs to be avoided like the plague! All this promotion of alcohol ,when was the last time you saw an advert on TV promoting good healthy organic food, or a water distiller, or anything else TRULY beneficial to our general well being? No its all Heineken, KFC, Coca Cola and people just LOVE it, the more junk the better. Eating and drinking crap to fill the void in their lives. Harsh maybe but I think if we're being honest with ourselves then this statement is quite accurate. It comes back again to self love, a person or society that loves itself does not self destruct and poison itself. Instead it looks after its health first and foremost rejecting toxins and poisons.

It's interesting when you actually sit and think about it how alcohol is associated with every kind of event in our lives. Weddings? Get drunk. Funerals? Get drunk. Birthdays? Get drunk? Weekend? Get drunk. The list goes on. Its become an addiction in society, not just in one Country but the World over, the irony is that we are PAYING to poison ourselves. Think about that for a minute, does that sound like sanity to you? God I wish I could claw back all the money I spent poisoning myself over the years, I could probably go on several nice holidays! Like I say Ive been no angel, I just opened my eyes and can now see it for what it is, something that inadvertently steals our freedoms by making us a much less functioning society.

# Chasing Pieces of Paper

Moving onto the ultimate World Religion now the, very glue that sticks slavery together and that is money. Here we have what is essentially a piece of paper that doesn't exist anywhere in Nature, of which its only value is that of what humans put on it themselves. Chasing these pieces of paper absolutely dominates not only our daily lives but more or less our entire existence. People will lie, steal, and even in some cases murder for more fake pieces of paper. Money, or lack of it keeps us in a survival scarcity mindset a constant 'fight or flight' mentality the perfect control mechanism for a force that seeks to dominate and control. What better way of diverting attention from your own wrongdoings than to get people running around like headless chickens after their slave notes day after day? Why doesn't anybody question this insanity?

It's one big scam even down to the fact that we have to PAY to exist here! I didn't sign up for this did you? Why aren't other intelligent life forms using pieces of paper to pay for their existence? To pay for their basic Natural rights of food, water, and shelter. Here's a clue maybe they are actually much more intelligent than us! Where are the monkeys, lions, elephants, and plants trying to accrue paper to justify their survival?

What is even more funny if it wasn't so tragic is that the World is in a 'crisis' because apparently there is a short supply of pieces of paper! Its not like they could just you know, print some more! No no you must work harder and pay more taxes because your Country is on the verge of a 'financial collapse'! I tell you what collapse we are on the verge of, a spiritual one. We have sold our souls down the river for money and its not even real! The banks are giving you nothing but fake numbers typed into a screen and then charging you interest on it, interest backed on nothing! If you walk into a bank and ask for a $10,000 loan they do not physically go and get you the $10,000 they just tap numbers into a computer. That is what youre paying all that interest for, for them to type numbers!

It doesn't matter what Country you go to in the World either, earning and chasing money will dominate their daily lives, billions of people probably dominating their daily thoughts too. Like I say money is the glue that sticks the rest of the bullshit together. Wars are fought because of money, weapons manufacturers reveling in it, and it makes no odds at all if people die. Drug and food companies completely disregard peoples health in order to make profit. It turns friends into enemies, it has fractured so many families right down the middle. In my older days working within Estate Agency I had people come into my branch and their mum or dad had not even been buried yet and they would be wanting to put their house on the market to get their greasy hands on the equity. Many arguments between family members would take place during the course of a house sale, arguments over who would get what, and what share. It used to sicken me then even before I knew the extent to which money rules our lives. It doesn't just control our minds but our very behavior to each other.

Just look at what happens to us if we don't pay this fake money back in terms of a loan or a mortgage etc. Big men are sent to our homes known as bailiffs to kick us out! Now they are increasingly accompanied by police who are normally armed these days and have no issues to help force this issue using violence, just because they missed a payment on something that doesn't exist, or were late. Where is the compassion from these banks? Like I say I have dealt with it first hand. The amount of times I would be sitting on somebody's sofa and they would be in tears because their husband had died or something and they couldn't afford to pay the mortgage, or they had been diagnosed with cancer and couldn't work. Did the banks care one bit? No of course not, sending threatening letters and bullies around to intimidate and scare people out of their minds. What a violent and heartless society this is, and yet again there are people willing to do the banks dirty work for them, harassing people all for a pay check. How on Earth could one sleep at night after evicting a family onto the streets is beyond me? It really is one big con. The idea of 'owning a home' when realistically it can be taken from you at any second. Some people will say yes but there are some people who take advantage when there are others that pay their way, well ok then what about the very financial institutes themselves that rip us off daily? Where is the blame for them and what they have done to families with their interest rises and financial crashes? Why don't you hold them responsible for anything? Where are their tax returns? Why is it that they can do whatever they want yet the finger gets pointed at some poor family that have got themselves into trouble with the rise in food, energy, and just the general cost of living? Its just another example of Stockholm syndrome protect the system and blame everyone else who struggles to function within it.

You know what I do not blame these so called 'free riders' of society either because they have been smart enough to realise its all a scam and they make sure the system works for them, they are intelligent enough to have worked out all the loopholes and I say good on them, that's what we should all be doing rejecting the bullshit! If we were all that smart then the system would cease to exist overnight. Non conformity is the only thing the system listens to and it only gets away with what it does because we participate all the time. Not only participating but taking pride in our participation. Get on the ladder and tie yourself down for the next 30 years so you cannot move anywhere. Interestingly enough when you look at the word mortgage in French broken down the word 'mort' means death, and 'gage' means pledge, literally the etymology of the word means death pledge!

Again the very idea that anyone can 'own' a piece of the Earth is quite frankly laughable in the first place. The land belongs to the Planet which belongs to Nature. Human beings in all of their wisdom have invented this concept that land can be divided up for 'ownership' and that these different sections of land can be 'bought and sold' using fake money. Yet in the UK you can actually buy up some land yet the government can say that you are 'not allowed' to live on your own piece of land you have just purchased! Im laughing as I type this because its all just so crazy and we just don't see it like that at all. How men in dark suits can dictate where somebody uses their free will choice as to where and how they live their life beggars belief, and again people will tell you that they are 'free,' of course that all ties in with them not wanting us to be self sufficient as we might then realise we don't need babysitters anymore. What they do want is folk cooped up in Cities (research Agenda 21) where the herds are funneled into huge concrete jungles where they serve the system all day long. Where they can drink in a wide array of pubs and have a constant stream of entertainment distracting them from what is really happening, because if we ever got to spend any length of time out in Nature (which after all is the closest to harmonic living we can get) then we may actually have time to ponder our own existence. So we are now at a stage where even if you own your own land you cannot live on it, oh my mistake you are 'allowed' if its some kind of temporary dwelling like a vehicle (at least in the UK you are, in the US your are not even allowed to live in your camper van on a permanent basis). Thanks government!

Another issue with housing are the sheer amount of empty properties just sitting there whilst there are more homeless people on the streets than ever before. In the UK there are almost one million empty homes which could easily house or provide temporary accommodation to people, especially in the freezing cold winter time. Why is this allowed to go on? Why is that acceptable? Are we that cold a society we just allow people to freeze and starve on the streets? Its not only the homes that are empty but the hearts of the banks who own them.

Interestingly enough going back to the whole money issue have you ever noticed how confusing they make the financial markets? Stocks, shares, inflation, interest rates, strengths and weaknesses of different currencies, the list goes on. Is this just one big charade to just confuse and cover up what is at its very core essence one big fake scam? To make it sound tangible? Make it look meaningful and complex to hoodwink the population into believing that there is any basis of realness to the whole thing. Money markets are often manipulated to benefit the few. People can and do make millions and billions from the rise and falls of market places and currency crashes. Whole societies can be plunged into deep despair as we saw in 2008. They can shape an entire population by 'crashing' something that is based on absolutely nothing, its the ultimate magic trick!

Any Country that looks to step away from the Rothchild central banking system can expect a huge amount of hostility, or as they like to call it 'freedom', from the west. Saddam Hussein wanted out, so too did Gaddafi. Both were heavily demonized by the western media propaganda machines. Indeed Gaddafi was idolized in Libya by his people and wanted to start a new African currency which would've helped put an end to poverty and hunger in that region. What happened was the west got wind of it and went in with a whole load of their 'liberation' and obliterated the place, and of course Gaddafi was murdered and the Countries financial system is still under control. Hussein was no angel granted but ask Iraqi people if life was better under his leadership before or after the West came in and the answer should speak for itself. One million people killed, seven million were forced to be rehomed, and that's without all the radiation left in the area from depleted uranium missiles which is now ensuring that there are now huge amounts of children being born with or developing cancer and causing disfigurements.

Iran has no central bank, North Korea and Venezuela also. Look at how those Countries have been demonized and sold as a threat for decades, and of course the most notable absentee is Syria who as I write this, we are trying to start a third World War with! This is about nothing more than control, complete control of the monetary system the World over, and once you get total control of that you get to control the people, nothing more and nothing less. This was never about liberation and we have to stop being so naïve to think that it is. If you have this kind of control you can then dictate the amount of abundance, poverty, or scarcity in a given society with ease.

Im not saying here that I don't need money to survive myself of course I do, I like everyone else am existing in this current paradigm where I have to earn these slave notes just like everybody else right now. Thinking ahead to a World without money perhaps there could be some kind of bartering system, or an exchange of goods or services. Clearly this could only happen in a truly conscious society where we were all working in unity and harmony together. I just know that money as it exists today is keeping us in servitude, we have no control over the market places and are powerless and left vulnerable to whatever they SAY has happened in regards to the latest boom or bust. The fundamental reason that some live in extreme poverty and others thrive is because of money, and this can never be a good thing.

Even things like a minimum wage. Think about that term, the bare minimum a company or corporation can get away with paying workers. How about a maximum wage? A cap on what bankers and politicians can earn, these people that have caused all this mess in the first place? But no we don't think about that, we watch TV programs like 'Benefits Street' who tell us to blame the poor people. It's the same with the whole tax avoidance argument centered around immigration. The amount of money lost to immigrants in taxes in comparison to the big corporations like Amazon, Starbucks, and McDonalds etc is microscopic, a mere drop in the ocean. All these companies with their off shore accounts in tax havens aren't contributing at all in that sense, but nobody thinks about that because there is no TV program telling them to blame the corporations. This is the point we are TOLD who is at fault all the time without actually working it out for ourselves. It seems to me people just want to hate on each other and they're not happy unless they have a gripe with one section of society, of course as long as it's not their owners! One thing that is guaranteed though is that the mainstream media will gladly fan the flames to ramp the animosity up as much as possible. People only hate because at some level they hate themselves. A person who understands that we are all in this together and has done the necessary inner work to at least like themselves doesn't carry that much hate in their hearts. Of course there are some immigrants that are bad but certainly not all of them, same with Muslims, Christians, Buddhists etc But what is a constant is the manipulation and evil taking place by the people that call the shots, yet the focus is never on them? Ultimately this debt based reality is at the root of it all, and we really need to start looking at money for what it truly is which is a form of control.

One of the fundamental issues here is how society views success. Success in most peoples eyes is not about gaining knowledge, serving others, spiritual evolution, or a deep understanding of the World around them. Society views success in terms of income bracket, what car youre driving, or how big your house is, and if you are unfortunate enough to have no job then you're not worth the shit on somebodies shoe! Think about it what is the first thing two people say when they meet apart from 'hello'? Its not what are your hobbies, goals, dreams, or what would you like to create? No its what do you do for a 'living' or what is your job? We truly love our servitude so much that it's the first subject we talk to each other about. Money ,what we do to earn it, and how much we have defines us and that cannot be right.

The same goes on a larger scale, a Country is not defined by how it helps its people, animals, or the environment, its value is only based on its GDP, or aside from that what resources can be extracted in order to gain more wealth. Literally everything is about value, materialistic value. It makes me laugh when I hear the term ' developed' and 'undeveloped' Countries. This so called 'developed' World is where a person may earn 50,000-100,000 pounds a year, yet has the vast majority of their wages taken (under the threat of violence) on taxes, and has to work a 60 hour working week for 50 weeks a year with just 2 weeks off to pursue other perhaps more soul fulfilling ventures? Doesn't sound very 'developed' to me. Ok you can argue that non developed Countries have it harder and yes many do, Im living in one now in Cambodia. Many folk are living off absolute peanuts, but do you know what they do have? A lot more unity, happiness and time for each other, they will help each other out, not always but oftentimes you will see them all pulling together. Western culture is materialistically and financially rich but spiritually it is dead. No care for anything other than chasing money.

These poorer Nations maybe poor wealth wise but at least they still have their souls intact and are not so consumed by greed. Spiritually they are much richer which begs the question who really is more developed? Why is it that people are kinder and give more when they have less? Ive seen clips where a homeless person has given up some of his pizza, and yet people in a restaurant in a similar experiment wouldn't give any to a person in need, or where the homeless person has been given a generous amount of money and given it away to someone pretending to need help, whereas the same experiment done with the average person won't give any away? Yet it's the people with nothing that we look down our noses at. My travels in life have found the same everywhere, the more material wealth oftentimes (not always) relates to less of a heart and visa versa.

How many people do you hear say that they want this or that? You hear it all the time in western society but how often do people NEED whatever it is they say they want? Is having the newest IPhone or gadget essential to your existence? Will blowing a few hundred pounds on a shirt or pair of trainers just because they are of a certain brand bring you happiness? Of course not we live way beyond our means, humans are not naturally supposed to live like this with a constant flow of trinkets that rape the Planet unnecessary of its resources. Most of us own way more than what we need, just turn up to a boot sale on a Sunday morning! There is so much wastage in comparison to others who have nothing in the World. This is not living in harmony with Nature . When you own so much it ends up owning you in the way of debt and the pressure you feel under to pay it all back, or even just in terms of clutter which is stressful in and of itself. Just ask the Japanese who practice Feng Shui to which there is a lot of truth, try it declutter I bet you will feel ten times better. I can say this as someone who used to own a lot, nice car, lots of clothes, and just unnecessary junk I didn't need but probably at some point bought on a whim thinking it would make me happy. As the years went by and I started finding happiness within so I sold almost everything I owned and now practice a minimalistic lifestyle and it feels great! I only buy what is absolutely essential these days, I don't have stuff everywhere, and I'm free to come and go as and when I please. I own a few clothes, a laptop (which I need for work) and a bed. No need to be stressing about paying things off on credit, for me this lifestyle is an expression of freedom. If I want to just up and leave to travel somewhere else then I can do that, and I feel like this minimalistic lifestyle reduces my footprint on the Earth and makes it softer, and whilst I still have a lot more than most poor people around the World I don't feel like I am rubbing it in their faces with owning lots of things that are unnecessary. I'm not telling people how to live here, and of course there are people with children who will be reading this who will struggle to live in such a way, I'm just pointing out the pitfalls of the human psyche of the whole take, take, take attitude or to put it another way, greed.

We can also extend this to food consumption where we are told that we need to eat three times a day, and that it is essential to healthy living, well any kind of research into the benefits of intermittent fasting (one meal a day) completely de bunks that theory. The results of not eating so much are remarkable, this is something that I have trialed myself and integrating into my own lifestyle on a more permanent basis. By eating one meal a day and resting your digestive system you are giving your body the chance to do the necessary housekeeping or dispel toxins from the body, and ultimately to give it a rest. When you eat three meals a day (normally quite heavily with meat) then your body is in a constant state of digestion with no time or energy to do anything else. Toxins build up in your cells over time and any repair work doesn't get done. I have experienced an abundance of energy, more clarity in thought, and the need for less sleep, all on just one meal a day. Of course the meal is high in nutritional value, but nevertheless my point is three meals are not essential to us like we have been led to believe.

This belief system extends to the consumption of meat, we are now swimming in evidence that eating the dead rotting carcasses of animals is not only bad for us, but it actually plays a massive role in the development of illnesses such as cancer, diabetes, and heart disease. Meat is very acidic and these diseases thrive in an acidic environment, keep your body in an alkaline state by eating a plant based diet rich in fruit, vegetables, nuts, beans, and grains and you create yourself a condition in your body where it is much harder for the diseases to take root. Of course we are not told this, there is way too much to lose in terms of money for the meat and dairy industry, which again are in bed with big pharma, or as I like to call it big harma! Even Cancer Research UK states that a vegan diet can reduce a person's chances of developing cancer by 85%, and vegetarian by 65%!

So these three meals a day filling yourself up with dead bodies is certainly not enhancing your health. The digestive tract and stomach are too small to eat meat and our teeth are certainly not those of a carnivore like a lion, it would be impossible for a person to rip into a live cow with their teeth like a true carnivore could, and then you would have to cook it to make it digestible, something else which when you stop to think about it isn't really a natutal thing to do. This all goes without mentioning the horrific treatment that goes on to the animals. Enslaved in cramped places, tortured, and then murdered just because humans 'like' the taste, and yet these same people will profess to 'love animals' whilst tucking into a steak for dinner! This is an oxymoron you cannot by definition 'love' something and have it killed to suit your tastebuds at the same time. How weird a World where we stroke and love our pets, yet have throats slit of cows, lamb, and chickens. It's just another case of want over need, the animals lives are their own and so are their products. We don't need to eat them, and in fact we thrive without them so can't we just leave animals alone in peace to live out their lives like we expect to live out our own?

The negative environmental impact of the meat and dairy industry cannot be ignored, the World's woodlands, rainforests, and jungles are being decimated at a horrifying rate to make way for cattle farming to meet a growing populations desire for flesh, and that's without all the fields needed to grow grain to feed these animals. The Oceans are also being overfished, it is estimated that by 2040 the Oceans will almost be devoid of fish, and they are also being polluted by all the animal faeces and wastage that gets pumped into them. It really is the elephant in the room in terms of what is harming our Planet more than anything else, but like I say don't expect the meat and dairy industry to fill you in on all this, they don't want you to see how much destruction meat eating does to the environment, it may hit their profit margins too hard.

When you mention this to people they generally just sweep it under the carpet, disregard it, or use some kind of mental gymnastics to justify it like carrots have feelings, and we're hunter gatherers, or you 'need' meat for protein which is another lie because there is actually more protein in a stick of broccoli than an entire steak! Obviously coming to the conclusion that they are in part culpable for the effect on the environment might mean they have to make the really uncomfortable change of quitting their meat, which let's face it most people would rather die than give up! Just because the 'natives ate meat' does it mean we have to? I mean aren't we supposed to be evolving here or are we supposed to be staying stagnant? If so we are the only species that does that. Like I have said before 'tradition' is half the time not always a good thing. A study of the Inuit tribes who live in the Arctic regions of Alaska, Canada, Siberia, and Greenland show clearly what a flesh eating diet does to the body, heart disease, respiratory problems, and cancer is rife and the average Inuit lives approximately 15 years less than their Canadian counterpart who will eat more of a balanced diet not relying solely on meat. And anyone talking about health whilst advocating meat eating is a fraud in my opinion and there are many out there. People who are supposed to be on the path of truth and justice still advocating barbaric behavior towards our animal cousins.

The whole 'plants have feelings' is not even an argument, firstly they do not have a central nervous system like animals. Animals are sentient beings meaning they feel emotions, get scared, love etc. They feel the emotions that humans feel. Spend some time stroking a cow and you will see for yourself, beautiful sensitive creatures yet look what we do to them. Plants, fruit, and vegetables do not try and run away screaming and crying when they are about to be killed, on the contrary they are offering themselves up like apples falling from a tree. We're not stuck on a desert Island either which is the other lame excuse you hear, we have a vast array of choices now as far as animal replacement products go, there is ALWAYS a cruelty free alternative to milk, meat, cheese, or eggs. Just in the UK last year veganism went up by something like 300% there is a huge array of tasty alternatives out there now. We are not going to starve without animal flesh, indeed we will thrive as I have seen with my own health. In my opinion vegans look younger and more vibrant which stands to reason because they are eating live food and not dead, so they will look more alive. Google 70 year old vegans they look 20 years younger than their actual age, so even for just purely shallow reasons it's worth considering giving it up!

This is of course without even touching on the karmic consequences involved. Is it really any wonder or coincidence that we find ourselves more enslaved, our energy literally being used as food to benefit those in control, when we are doing exactly the same to others? 'What you do to others will be done to you' springs to mind, and expecting to be free ourselves whilst enslaving and murdering others is really just the height of ignorance and hypocricy in a place where man has put himself on the pedestal as God. There is a need for greed where we are taking all the time, including things we have no right to be taking. The wastage is huge, a waste of resources, the Natural World, and the lives of billions of land animals every year. Im not telling people what to do with their dietary choices, although obviously I have a clear bias, but moreover presenting the WHOLE picture of what is involved with this industry and the footprint it leaves because like I say, the whole picture is never given to us. The brutal truth is our eating habits are killing not only ourselves but the Planet, and from there we all have a personal decision to make as to if we want to support that.

# Truth Mixed With Lies

When you deeply research these systems of control or belief systems that have been structured into the human mind you come to realise in fact that many times there is always an element of truth into what is being said, this is very clever and devious mind manipulation when you really pay attention. There are many 'wolves in sheep clothing' out there to sway public opinion, or gather some kind of momentum to insert ideas into human consciousness. This is of course extremely prominent in politics where more often than not to get people 'onside' the given politician will say a huge amount of what people WANT to hear, they will speak a large amount of truth in some cases, then at the final hour there is a complete swing to the other direction. A recent example of this was with the Labour party leader in the UK Jeremy Corbyn who we are told at least, spent the vast majority of his time as a politician campaigning for the UK to leave the EU, this of course made him extremely popular amongst voters, and he certainly comes across as the proverbial 'nice old man' who just wants peace in the World yet what happened? At the 11th hour he encouraged his sways of followers to vote to stay in Europe! This is what happens time and again with politicians, people would not have been interested in him if he had shown his true colors at the start given the mood in the UK at the time. He had to garner support by saying the right things, but of course his agenda was the opposite all along in that he wanted to encourage people to stay. His support listened to him, they trusted him, they hang off of his every word. He plays 'good cop' then leads people down a cul de sac at the last minute. Same with these new celebrity 'saviors' like Russell Brand who is having a large influence in politics particularly with young people these days. He did the same thing as Corbyn when it came to the general election, encouraged people not to vote because it was all a farce, then again at the last minute told everyone to vote labor! The reason for this is that these people come from the system themselves, they are part of it. They simply serve the agenda the bankers, the corporations, and the people behind the scene pulling the strings. How often to politicians SAY they are going to do something and then they do the complete opposite? They are nothing more than mere actors and actresses.

It's the same with Religions the odd truth thrown in as bait to get the masses hooked, yet it is built on a sea of lies, or at least based on allegories that have an element of truth in them. Used so people constantly give their power away to a bearded man sitting on a cloud thinking they have no power themselves, and to abstain from taking any self responsibility and leaving everything into the hands of 'God' to sort out so they certainly won't rise up to make any positive changes themselves. This is also rife with the increasingly popular 'New Age' or spiritual movement. When you delve deep into it there is a hell of a lot of truth in it, truth about our true spiritual nature, our abilities to create and manifest our desires, the power of our mind and thoughts etc. This is all very true but it is also full of deceptions and one way streets leading to cul de sacs, which if taken seriously can mislead millions of people. Ideologies such as 'just accept everything' or 'never get angry' or 'focusing on the negative will bring you more negative' all these concepts are the very REASON as to why the World is as it is. It just promotes complete avoidance over things that matter. I highly recommend people watch Mark Passio's presentation on YouTube called 'New Age Bullshit' here he outlines all of this in such depth so you can clearly see where the deceptions lie. We should only be 'accepting' things that cannot be changed, and we should get angry over what is happening here, the emotion of anger exists for a REASON and that is to drive us to change a situation. Of course dwelling in anger all the time is not beneficial either but to say 'never get angry' is to deny us of something that was created within us for a specific reason. It's why all the other emotions exist like guilt for example, it's a feeling of maybe we need to go and correct a particular situation in order to heal it. The one that gets me is that we MUST 'destroy our ego'. Well I'm sorry what other being in Nature sets out to destroy an aspect of itself? The ego is what helps people go out and create in the World. Where would all the music, artistry, and comedy be if there were no ego, it's what makes us individuals, it's part of our personality. It helps us express our own individual blueprint onto the World. Now I'm not saying we should be completely stuck in ego, no of course the ego needs to be harnassed as it can most definitely get out of control, it should be used as a tool to get through life, certainly not obliterated like the New Age would have you believe, a World where everyone accepts everything, is never angry, and never expresses their personality, no thanks that doesnt sound like too much fun to me, although it would certainly make the population easier to control which is exactly the reason why it is propagated in the first place.

The word we have to fall in love with again is 'discernment' we need to really analyze and feel people and the information they are putting out there, and go back and question these age old traditions and rigid belief systems and ask who does it benefit? We fall for anything anyone says these days, its really frustrating to see how naïve people are because its happening constantly, the way we are so easily manipulated has to stop and that means we have to take a step back and think before jumping in head first into something. All it takes is a few good lines from a politician and people are sold, they listen to empty words instead of ACTIONS which should always be the way we judge a person and their intent. Its like we never learn either, falling for the same tricks and lies over and over again. Its like we are so desperate to believe our masters are 'good' that there is like a mental schism taking place whereby we completely bypass the discernment process. We have to realise that everything, or at least most things coming from the system will first and foremost benefit the system itself. People will come to 'represent us' who appear, at least on the surface, as a good genuine person, but in reality they are batting for the other team. Look at the outgoing President of the United States Barack Obama, incredibly polished at looking kind and compassionate, he even gets his hankie out at times to wipe away the crocodile 'tears' yet here is a man that has had no problem in dropping bombs on poor people every 20 minutes for 8 years! And to maintain the illusion of the 'good guy' has even unbelievably been awarded a Nobel Peace Prize! You literally couldn't make it up. We have to start thinking critically, we have to forget how a particular person makes us FEEL for a second with words and look at what their actions are. There are simply nowhere near enough people doing this. Its like taking candy from a baby for these people who prey on our naivety and constant obsession to look for someone to lead us, giving both our energy and power away.

One of the most prominent underlying issues to all of this is that people are looking up to the state as the parent. Is the State playing that parental role which is now so often missing in many peoples lives these days? Perhaps the State for women represents the so often missing father figure or that someone to look after them, it stands to reason why more women are turning to government to be the 'protector' when the men are not operating from their masculine core as I have discussed already. People seem to be quite comfortable in the system as it represents the false sense of security that people haven't had in their own upbringing. As we know divorce rates are through the roof these days and its very difficult to find anyone at all that doesn't come from a broken home. Many people are broken from their childhoods and are looking to the State to fix that, literally taking the place of the abandoned parent.

It's extremely interesting when you delve deep into the mindset of society, there are certain trends and trains of thought going on deep within people which make them feel so reliant on government. I guess it always come back to self and owning your own power which can only ever be done by healing ourselves one by one. Its certainly an ongoing process but as a person becomes more healed they start to become more empowered, then eventually they will come to the realization that they have always had that power, and eventually that desire to want to be governed will fall away, it really is about mentally growing up for us all.

I think so many of us go through life, and I have done so before myself, papering over the cracks of our minds. Patching up traumas and childhood issues with temporary bandages like drugs, alcohol, and junk food, which ultimately end up escalating those issues. So we have a population of people walking around with all kinds of baggage which has mentally weakened them so they effectively don't have the strength to even consider living without owners. We are not responsible for what happened to us in our childhoods however we are responsible for what we carry forward into our lives. We have to realise that these temporary fixes are making our problems worse, both individually and collectively. Its about taking responsibility and stepping out of the victim mentality that has infested our society.

Of course its not easy and my intention is not to demean peoples issues, some people's lives have been truly horrific, however I don't think there exists anyone on the Planet who has had a trouble free life, I mean that is part of the experience of even being human, it's the highs and lows and the ebbs and flows that make it so interesting. I know people who have managed to turn their lives around after unbelievable circumstances so it can be done no matter how bad we think our situations are. There is that saying 'heal ourselves and the World will start to heal' I don't think truer words have been spoken. We have to face our shadows and go back to the root cause of what is holding us back. Introspection, meditation, talking, and going back into our inner child, whatever it may take we owe it to ourselves to become the best version of ourselves. We can be healed if we want it enough, and of course if we develop the courage to do so. Its truly remarkable as to what human beings are capable of, our will and spirit is immense if properly applied. We hold the power within us and its about time we start realizing it. Waking up to our true power to overcome the most grueling of challenges is the ultimate solution. Know it, to the person reading this know it to your core just how strong you are and all those years of negative self talk are just lies you keep telling yourself!

When talking about mental health I honestly think people suffer so much because they are not doing what their soul truly desires, deep down they are crying out, they are in anguish. Their free spirit and innate creativity has been smashed out of them as soon as they were able to walk almost, taught to obey, never question authority, sitting in a classroom being told what to think and what to believe, then straight onto work more often than not doing something that their soul deep down despises. The soul is directed form a very young age onto this familiar path, is it any wonder that so many people feel lost and unhappy when that inner child has been lost also, that creative aspect of us that has been beaten down? The explorer, the writer, the philosopher, and the artist. Imagine a World where we were free to truly walk our own paths, how many could honestly say they would still do the same thing as they are doing now? For me a large part of societies collective mental problem comes from the suppression of the TRUE self and our very souls, a basic inability to both express and live out its true wants and needs. Our souls are held in cages so how can we ever expect to be really deeply happy and content? We're told to 'shut up and sit down' from childhood and in reality this goes on right through to adulthood. I know this to be the case because I lived it, I hated school and then went onto do jobs that were extremely unfulfilling and deep down they drained my soul energy. The material gains like a nice house and car etc really only masked the suffering that was going on inside of me. Somewhere deep down I knew that I was only existing, I was not living, and certainly not living my purpose. What I really wanted was to set my soul on fire, to do what it was that I had come here to do, and that's all any of us really want, just to live in line with that spark within, that reason that gets us out of bed in the morning.

Following our passions in life is essential for happiness, and yet there are very few brave enough to follow their hearts. People take so called 'security' over taking risks that may reap longer term happiness. Taking a job that may offer more 'financial security' yet spiritually will leave them dead because deep down its not really what they want to be doing. Again Ive done it, Ive worked in banks previously because it was 'safe' yet it was like going in and watching paint dry day after day! I always say to young people follow your heart, even if it means taking the more risky road, at least you will have no regrets even if it doesn't work out. The Universe loves courage and Ive found that by following my own heart, albeit later on in life, the Universe has put certain people, places, and circumstances in my path to help me achieve what my heart desires it was just a case of taking that leap in the first place.

I really resent the system for stealing my creativity for all those years, and its only now that I have the time that I realized I could even write and how much I enjoy it! I never had a moments peace to write before, any free time I had was spent exhausted and trying to recover from a stressful day or week at work. Its astounding how much of our true selves are stolen from us, our most valuable commodity our time is used up mainly doing things that we don't want to be doing. So its easy to see the root cause of so much unhappiness and emptiness in the World. I encourage anyone who is procrastinating and who these words resonate with to go out and find yourself, find your passion, your reason for existing, then follow it. Take the risks necessary to get you there and you will find as I have in my own life that if you follow that calling, that feeling, then you will get help from something higher. Take a leap of faith and have no regrets. Time passes by so quickly, leave your mark on the Planet and do what you came here to do which is to express and honor your true self and all your passions and desires. Strive for greatness in whatever field excites you, give it your all.

We have fallen in love with average, existing, and just getting by, its time to end this relationship and have a better one with ourselves, one where we honor our own individual greatness within. No more 'little me syndrome' victim mentality, and this blame culture that we live in. Everyone wants to blame somebody or something else for their own fuck ups, society does the same. If its not the bankers, it's the politicians, or the Muslims. How about we all look in the mirror and realise our lives are shaped and turn out the way they do because of us, and collectively its the same. Its our very lack of care and action that the World is as it is. We don't take any responsibility, we just want to leave it up to others to sort out and nothing ever gets done. Individually there are only so many years that we can play the victim before the years have passed away and we realise we haven't moved any further forward because we have been constantly blaming others. Life is a test we are all constantly being tested over and over again, and it just boils down to whether or not we want to pass those tests. Bad habits have been passed down from generation to generation, when exactly are we going to throw a spanner in the works and intervene?

Which generation will be the one to shake things up for a new paradigm to take place? I honestly think it has to be this generation, the last one to have experienced any kind of freedom as it continues to be bled dry. Lets look at our fuck ups square in the face, realise that a lot of what we have been led to believe is in fact bullshit, what we have allowed to be created here is bad, take responsibility for it and do our upmost to turn the situation around for the upcoming generations. The Native Americans and their thinking and planning in terms of seven generations ahead, that is the epitome of TRUE care. What of this generation? Do people even care about their own one that they are existing in currently? Lets stop blaming and start acting.

Most of the time we are lying to ourselves about so much, and people will SAY they like honesty and truth yet they hate it when you speak it! Another George Carlin quote 'The World is glued together by bullshit' could it be that this is just a reflection of what is going on within all of us? Can we really expect to live in an honest and truly free World when we aren't even honest with ourselves? As within so without, as above and so below. Change starts with each and everyone of us, like I say when you are honest with yourself and start to heal then a part of the World is healed also. Little by little we can start turning things around, yet by blaming others it automatically puts us in victim mode and in a position of disempowerment.

## Solutions

From the very outset of this book I stated that by pointing out the problems also indicates where many of the solutions lie, this is not rocket science as it's simple in the fact that we just need to STOP doing a lot of what we have done up until this point. In many cases very little action or even no action is needed its just a case of discerning the truth then operating and most importantly acting upon what you know. We don't need whole new systems, that's just papering over the cracks because its not going to the root cause of what has led us to this point which is a large part down to our behavior, ignorance, and naivety.

Firstly any we need to open our minds to the fact that there is an awful lot going on around us that might not be true, and that actually there is much more to this reality and existence than this physical 3D realm we see in front of us. There are many dimensions operating within the same space that we just cannot see, as humans we are are basically blind as to what is out there as we only operate from the five senses, and are locked into a tiny fraction of what is going on by our visible sight, our sight doesn't even give a quarter of what is really going on around us, and especially when it comes to understanding energy. Everything is energy at its core and it vibrates at different speeds to give the impression of solidity, yet it is our brain that perceives it to be solid. Any study of quantum physics will tell you that energy is not matter it is literally empty space! That ultimately is what we are dealing with a reality where everything around us is permeated by source energy. Until we get to grips that this is not just a PHYSICAL reality we will not begin to understand the World around us at large.

So the manipulation runs so much deeper than just the physical level its also going on metaphysically and on a cellular level (which is for another book!) We have up until now only been perceiving what is possible from a five sense perspective, yet there is infinitely more going on! Even mainstream science admits now that quantum physics is very real. So we need to open our minds to the multidimensional Universe that we are operating in, and that we are not just physical. We are so much more, human beings are extremely powerful, abundant in our ability to create and manifest, our very hearts are huge powerful vortexes which is why it is always under attack. Waking up to our true SPIRITUAL Nature, who we REALLY are, and understanding that we are so much more than what we have been told is key. We are in this World but not of it. Your spirit and soul never die, your physical body might but then you at your core essence will go on, so really when you look at it from a higher point of view, is there really anything to be that frightened of? We live in so much fear because we believe that we are mortal when in reality this is just an experience of probably countless that we have had before, its just another space suit in which we have chosen to observe, learn, and grow. You are not 'little me' at your very core you are a genius, you have just forgotten it, and its time to remember.

You are not just one person and you CAN make a difference. What you do here will send ripples not just throughout the World but throughout the Universe. That is what the very word is telling you that YOU have the Universe inside of you! A spark of the creator dwells inside of you and you think you're just a nobody?! Come on its over now, step into your power today and start casting stones into the pond, and then watch those ripples turn into waves as just by being you, it will inspire others to do the same. All those times people have told you, or that you have felt insignificant these were all lies. Break free from caring about what others think about you and express your TRUE self. They may hate you for it but ultimately it is because they wish they were you. They wish they had your courage to step outside of the sheep pen. Time to go and be the lion that you were born to be!

I've spoken about three key words extensively in this book already, they really are at the heart of any kind of solution, the three go together and once we activate all three within us we will be getting somewhere. They are care, courage, and imagination. To even make a start on the road of truth and freedom requires the first aspect in abundance because you have to care enough about what is going on around you to even start knowledge seeking, it's the first point of call. In reality you cannot make somebody care, I know because Ive been trying for years! You can lead a horse to water as it were but that person has to activate the care aspect in their own consciousness and heart. Personally I will never understand people that don't care, it's the thing that hurts me the most, more than the manipulation itself. They either care or they dont its their choice but that's where it starts.

The next part is caring enough to the point where you are willing to take action in the World and do something about the situation which is where the next quality of courage comes in. You can have all the knowledge in the World but unless you have the balls to go out and express what you know in some way then you may aswell stay asleep to everything. The World doesn't need anymore cowards there are more than enough already for me. For me there is only one worse thing than ignorant people, and its people who know what is happening and are willfully sitting on the sidelines doing nothing as others are left to do the dirty work. Scared and living in fear of what their mum, wife, friends, teacher, or government thinks of them. Who are you as a human being if you stand idly by and allow all this to go on around you? What we need are more warriors, people who are willing to step outside of fear despite what others may think of them. That is true courage, to feel fear but do it anyway. Fear just feeds into the parasites that like to keep us in that mindset and vibration. Does is mean making sacrifices? Yes. Does it mean some people disliking you? Yes. Does it even mean you giving your life? Well if we are serious about change then it is also a resounding YES. Ironically the more you put yourself out there the more help, support, and protection you get from the Universe and if there is one thing it loves its courage. Its your choice are you going to be another nobody that stands for nothing, or are you one of the few people that actually stands up for something these days?

Of course these two qualities mean nothing without the third which is imagination. It doesn't have to be this way, humans can be much better than what we have become. There doesn't always have to be war, poverty, and suffering. We can transcend these times and we can create Heaven on Earth, we have to open up that right side of the brain which we have been shut off from and start to imagine that this is completely possible. We have to first be able to imagine a World without the belief in authority, where there is this constant search for leaders to run our lives for us, we don't need another psychopath or wolf in sheep clothing calling the shots. There would be no more chaos than there already is, and even that would be temporary as we find our feet. This system needs to be purged not only from our existence but from our very mentality. It really is time for the for the TRUE meaning of anarchy to come to the party where nobody rules but we rule ourselves.

Given time humanity can thrive without this parasitical entity we call government leeching from us all the time. To imagine a World without authority making immoral laws that they don't even obey themselves is to start that very manifestation process, everything starts in the mind and if enough people even start thinking along these lines then the Universe will rearrange itself to give us the circumstances in which to move forward in this direction. Clearly its not an overnight job and it certainly wont be easy, but anything with great benefits is rarely easy. When was anything great achieved by taking the easy road? So many of these solutions are based in our mental programming so it is that part we need to work on, our very diseased psyche's, rather than going out protesting or rioting in the streets which of course plays right into their hands with their police state ready and waiting to be enforced along with the water cannons! Care, courage, and imagination are the keys to unlocking our current situation.

Clearly nothing will also be achieved whilst we are at each others throats. Continuing to blame Muslims, the poor, or black people etc for our troubles is counter productive, we need to realise who the common enemy is and stop buying into the deliberate 'divide and rule' propaganda. We need to come together as one human family all religions, races, colors, and creeds in unison. Wow what a beautiful scenario that would be! It doesn't matter which Country you are from, we all face the same problems to a more or lesser degree, we are weak when we are divided that's why so much is done to keep us that way as I have already written about. We need to wake up to that agenda and realise we are being played.

I would suggest organising small meetings in your town or City, get to know your neighbours and help each other out, look up from the mobile phones and make an effort to talk to that Muslim or gay person, are they really that bad? Are they really a threat to you? Or is it more the people who steal half your wages each month costing you much more than any immigrant coming in that you have been told to hate on? If you are still in hate mode could it be that you still need to work on yourself and are projecting something you actually feel about yourself? We are all one consciousness so the idea of separation is quite hilarious, lets stop fighting amongst ourselves and grow up. We need to stop acting like kids in a playground because the bullies rule here! Isn't it interesting how children don't know the difference between race, color, or creed? Ok on a physical appearance level they might but they don't hate over it, hate is learnt or taught so who is doing the teaching? If they see and hear hate everywhere then of course they will be a product of that hate filled society and its collective mindset, it has to end if we are to stand a chance.

If we are to decentralize then as I mention organising between ourselves is vitally important, even to just start on a small scale. There is nothing quite like getting a room of likeminded people together, the atmosphere is buzzing. Bringing people together who all want the same thing is very powerful, and if anything was to ever go badly wrong then its important we have people we now to support us. This is what we need to do we need to rely on each other and ourselves making strides forwards in groups and communities just like the Native tribes do. If there is no meeting in your area then start one yourself, even if just one or two people show up don't wait for someone else to organize something, be the change yourself. Working out how we can become more sustainable, how we can improve things, how to help others we have to start with our own areas first and foremost. The problem that I have experienced first hand is that people want others to lead, they want others to organize, so nothing ever happens or gets done. People seem to like sitting around and just moaning about things without actually going to do something positive about it. If everyone around the Country starting organising and arranging small meetings we wouldn't need governments because we would be relying upon ourselves and this has to be a huge part of the solution.

Moving onto the media, I was going to sum this up in just one sentence 'turn it all off.' We have to remember that the State owns the media and the State always has an agenda it will use the media heavily as a tool of manipulation, for example where does all the spreading of hate and division start? In the media, and its propagated 24/7 year after year. When was the last time you saw a story when a Muslim and a Christian came together for a common cause (because it happens a lot believe it or not?) When was the last time you heard anything from the media that wasn't based in fear? As I've discussed in length the tell-lie-vision is not your friend, not if you want to live in the real World. Turn it off, don't buy the newspapers or anything, or maybe just if you just want to keep an eye on the lies and where they want to take the agenda. The media is dying there is huge mistrust these days and for good reason, don't be part of its last weak heartbeats. As I have discussed we have to rediscover and fall in love with that word 'discernment' and that is difficult to do when we are being bombarded with their version of everything, we need to listen to that gut feeling, or the higher mind as it were. Don't even listen to me, discern what I am saying and see and feel if it resonates as truth.

Also stop paying for things that make you feel worse like women buying the glossy, airbrushed magazines that put you down and tell you that you're not good enough. The women of this World are going to show this Planet back home with their love, care, and nurture. You are powerful beyond measure and already beautiful! None of us are insignificant or worthless and we need to remember who we really are. If you listen to the media your feedback will only ever be that you have no power, nothing can ever change, and we must rely on the system at all times, and the so called 'leaders'.

One of the reasons we find ourselves in this position is because we constantly want to give our power away. We live in a blame culture where its always someone else's responsibility. Nobody wants to take any action as I touched on earlier. It is my view that each and everyone of us has a moral obligation to help make this World a better place. Its time to stop looking at others to do all the dirty work, its not down to just one person or a small group of people its about all of us, we are all in this together. If you are in awareness of what is happening here then you have to act, this really isn't time for people to be sitting on the sidelines as spectators.

This self responsibility spans over many subjects, take health for example it is your responsibility to look after your health and not your doctors. If you want to eat a bad diet and not exercise then don't be surprised when your body starts to shut down or you get some kind of disease, running to the doctors to get a pill is not going to solve all of your problems. Also think about the people that have to pick up the pieces of your lack of care if you do become ill? What situation does that then put others around you who will care for you? Its quite selfish in my opinion. Taking responsibility is about being honest with ourselves in both our personal lives and in World issues, but its starts with us ultimately. Is what we are eating good for us, the animals, or the Planet? If not then should we be doing it? Of course I'm just using health as an example here, it relates more than anything when you are talking about a belief in authority and government which I have written about extensively. If you're happy to allow others to run and dictate your lives then expect to be taken advantage of. That is government in a nut shell, a force that is given so much power because humans are still waiting to realise their own. Continuing to look to men in dark suits for answers and solutions is a recipe for disaster. The World is in complete chaos because we consistently hand our power over to them.

There are no excuses anymore there is not one Country certainly that Im aware of that is not entrenched in corruption, maybe the exception of Iceland who really did show the World what can happen when they took their own power back, they came together in unison and threw out the bankers, they took control of their Country again so it can be done. A Country that was on its knees financially is now starting to thrive again, its not without its problems of course, but it just shows you what we are capable of when we unite. These people are destroying our Planet and sadly in many cases raping our children, so why on Earth would we give any power to them? Giving up the belief in authority and reclaiming your own sovereignty has to be up there at the top of all solutions. Self responsibility also comes with looking outside of ourselves for a savior, we are far too quick to put people on pedestals if they say the right things now and then. We have to be our own saviors, we are the solution that we have been waiting for. Same goes for traditions we need to revaluate our whole belief systems, in fact we should aim to be in a place where we have no rigid belief systems, that's not to say that we cant ever know anything, only that we question the ideas and concepts we have grown up with, we need to open our minds take a step back and look at everything again objectively. Does what we believe in keep us from looking outside ourselves or does it promote empowerment and internal sovereignty?

Conscious parenting for me is a huge area and I certainly don't have all the answers all I know is that kids are growing up going through the same systems, being taught the same old indoctrination, and not really learning anything of value. A blanket statement is necessary here in that a lot of parents are mentally and spiritually childlike themselves, and are attempting to raise children from that basis. I don't see many children being taught on the laws of morality, how to be happy, proper nutrition, the connection to Nature or the natural World in general. All I see if I'm honest is parents packing their kids off for indoctrination each day and then sitting them in front of the TV or Ipad when they get home. Then we wonder why the cycle repeats itself over and over again. Most kids are vaccinated up to the eyeballs making them unhealthy and are then running to the doctors to get dose upon dose of pills and antibiotics without ever connecting the dots. Parents have to start taking responsibility and raising more conscious children, home schooling is a huge one for example. To allow a completely immoral system which is sinking in its own lies to educate our young is beyond madness. I'm sure its not easy to homeschool but I know many people who have found a way of doing so. Giving a child the chance to think freely and form their own opinions, and to teach them REAL empowering information surely is the best start they could have in life.

Obviously feeding them a constant supply of sugar and Happy meals is not helping them on their journey through life either, raising them to eat junk as an adult too. Im no expert by any means but there are certain things I know I would never do. I think we generally don't give children enough credit, they already hold so much knowledge, their minds are pure because they have just come from source, and generally we fill those pure minds with just utter junk from schooling, TV, traditions, and religions.

If we are to evolve we have to end the cycle of one generation after another doing exactly the same thing yet expecting different results. These times require brave parenting, parents who are willing to take the flack from other parents for stepping outside of the norm. Surely our children deserve the very best in life to ensure they are on the right path otherwise what is the point of having them in the first place? Children being born now are already advanced, they are here with a heightened awareness, they can handle a lot more than we give them credit for. Raising conscious children means helping the World become more conscious.

The harsh truth is that we have kids having more kids, not much thought or pre planning is going on, people complain that they can't afford this and that, it's not easy to homeschool etc but surely if that's the case then why would you have them in the first place if you're not in a position to give them the very best start? It sounds brutal but it doesn't make it any less true. Why do parents feel so much pressure from other parents? Who cares what other parents are doing? Chances are what they are doing has come directly from what they saw someone else doing, or have been told is the right thing to do. I will never understand that, all that should matter is the best for the child, and if that means taking some verbal abuse or ridicule from other parents then so be it. This has to be a generation that bucks the trend and it is this generation of parenting that will have a huge influence on how the future turns out. Are we just going to churn out another generation of unquestioning sheep, TV watchers who contribute very little to existence, or are we going to raise them as spiritual powerhouses that are going to be a shining light and help change this place?

Staying healthy is a big middle finger to the system, much is done to keep us stupid and dumbed down so that we don't even have the capacity to want to effect any kind of change. Poor quality and artificial food, soft drinks, and alcohol is bombarded on us daily through media and advertisements. To be healthy is to help our minds think clearer and with more clarity. If our bodies are in good shape then we feel better and if we feel better then we stay out of the lower vibrational energy that they want us to stay in. I could write another book about health, what to eat and what not to eat, but lets face it its mainly common sense its not rocket science. What we put into us is what we get out. A population of healthy people capable of critical thinking is not what they want at all, and a hell of a lot harder for them to control. By not looking after ourselves we are playing right into their hands, when we are weak we are easily manipulated. It's the same with the pharmaceuticals, before rushing down to the Dr's to get a 'quick fix' pill (which even has the word 'ill' in it) which will probably do more damage than good in the long run anyway, have a look at what Nature has to offer, there is an abundance of natural alternatives all easily researched online. Ok they may not give you the quick fix, papering over the cracks feel good factor until another ailment pops up, but the longer term deeper healing will stand much more chance of getting done properly. We come from Nature ourselves so its completely unnatural to think that synthetics or even worse radiation is going to produce any long term benefits for us. Research for yourself and become your own doctor.

We can change things not by voting but with our choices. Stop buying crappy food and they will have to start selling good organic produce, there is more and more selection everyday now in supermarkets. If we demand the alternative then the greed driven mentality of these corporations will have to supply it. Health truly is wealth and we can no longer trust these people to provide what we need. Including regular detoxifications, drinking quality water, juicing, exercising regularly, yoga, and meditation are all wonderful ways of living, but it begs the question why would you want to live any other way? Self love starts with our bodies. To evolve and change things we must be able to function effectively in the first place, we have to start connecting the dots in terms of our quality of food and the massive increase in chronic illnesses. Again it's a case of stopping what we have been doing that has made us weak in the first place.

Clearly the best food we can eat is that which we have grown ourselves and there are more and more people doing this as they now realise the system controlling the food supply is not a good idea, self sustainability is where we need to look to next, it is in effect the ultimate rejection of control, even if we can look to do it in part. All I know is that the more we can step away from them and stand on our own two feet the less power they hold over us, and the less time we need to spend slaving away for them. The more we rely on them for everything the more strength they have. I spoke earlier of the havoc alcohol causes in society, just imagine how much smoother and peaceful things would run without this poison? The glorification of poisoning oneself has to end. Surely we can do better and we owe it to ourselves and future generations to become the very best versions of ourselves. In my opinion its no good just knowing things, we have to walk the walk in line with what we know as much as possible.

There are no need for riots here, its doesn't have to get to that stage. The solution lies in the negative which is saying no. As we reject more and more manipulations they simply wont work anymore, and things will change further to our favor. We are seeing this more and more with small victories scattered all over the place as people are now starting to put their health in their own hands and rejecting mainstream medicine. People are starting to reject things like TV licenses now because they don't want to pay for their own brainwashing, the system cannot handle mass numbers saying no, yes it might send threatening letters designed to keep you in fear but there is just simply too many of us rejecting it now. Imagine this on a larger scale if everyone suddenly decided to stop paying their taxes one day, there would be nothing they could do! We need to realise that through our sheer numbers we have the power and always have done, its just we have been so divided throughout the years, this constant division through the media to stop the very unity I am writing about here. If we all woke up one morning and decided to say no to all of this then the World would change quickly, of course Im not expecting for things to happen that way, I see this as more of a gradual process with small victories leading up to a larger one along the way.

A big show of non compliance has to come from the public over Wars. The very fact it is so glorified and celebrated openly beggars belief. The need to stop supporting this organized murder is long overdue, a World without War will only manifest itself once we completely reject it and stop buying into the constant lies from the only people that ever seem to want it. We have to stop looking at War, and those who fight in it as 'heroic' in fact the opposite is true, I don't see how dropping bombs on small villages on somebody elses orders as heroic at all! War is no joke, and being accepting or indeed buying into the glorification of it is not only horrific in and of itself, but it also makes us complicit. If we cannot see that War has never achieved anything by now then we deserve this cage that we are living in. Im personally tired of 3 or 4 days every year where people get all worked up and sentimental about the military. Im also tired of walking around my local town and seeing recruitment days for young boys, and even the parents encouraging it, in fact it makes me feel sick, this is the type of brainwashing that needs to be rejected wholeheartedly. So it really falls onto the soldiers that are doing the fighting, it is no longer acceptable to say 'I was just following orders' or people die because of 'collateral damage' these are no longer excuses, and they never were. All support for military and War in general needs to be withdrawn, and these soldiers need to join the REAL war which are direct attacks on their OWN people by western governments with poisons in the food, air, and water supplies (all easily researchable, with chemtrails being sprayed from the sky). Where are the F16s taking down these chemtrail pilots who are spraying down aluminium and barium onto our children? Where are the soldiers ransacking parliament to arrest paedophile politicians who pay no taxes? I personally want 'protecting' from all that! So it is going to take a huge shift in mindsets, and thankfully there are many military personal now waking up to the manipulations and realizing that they have been hoodwinked, these ex soldiers speaking out are the REAL heroes and have my upmost respect. They have been extremely brave in acknowledging the fact that it was all a lie, and instead of living in denial are trying to make up for what has happened. We need to encourage this, and support these ex soldiers. They need to understand that they will not be vilified by the public as long as they side with truth. We need them now more than ever to join the good fight, but firstly they need them to see what they are doing is wrong, and if they don't see it, it is down to us to make them see it. I honestly believe that one day humanity will look back at war with shock and horror, in that it wont believe that it ever allowed it to happen. 'Its always been this way' will not wash anymore, EVERYONE needs to get on the field of battle and express this unapologetically. In a nut shell down tools, say no, put down the weapons and let those that want War fight themselves.

Peaceful non compliance as much as we can, turning the screw one way on their control mechanisms as they try and turn it the other way. The ultimate battle between good and evil, whose side are you on? Are you still going to advocate all of this madness for generations to come, or are you going to step out of the indoctrination and mind control that has been imposed on you ever since you were a kid and were given a toy gun to play with to normalize violence? Because that how far back it goes, you were born thinking this is normal, its not and it never will be? I dont have all the solutions, Im just someone who woke up one day and saw the World for what it truly is, and Im concerned all I know is it starts with each and everyone of us giving a fuck. We have such a beautiful Planet here, people in general in their true selves are loving, caring, courageous, and peaceful. We all want to live in peace and to be left alone, and for others to be left alone, to be free to pursue our hearts desires, to create, and to live lives free from struggle and fear. That is how life should be for all of us, living in harmony with each other, and coming together as one human family. We have to hold that vision in our minds because that is how life should be like, and it can be like that again. We are at a crossroads as a species, we either go deeper into the abyss, or we can turn the situation around to the point whereby we are no longer just existing, but we are living. Not just for ourselves but for our children and grandchildren.

## Self-Publishing Your Book
## Made Easy!

Sazmick Books offer self-publishing and marketing services to authors of most genres. We help to fulfill your ambition of getting your work from typed or written manuscript, into a printed book or E-book with customisable add-ons.

Simple packages, Stunning books.
Chat with us and get your book on the road today!

# www.sazmickbooks.com

**For All Your Self-Publishing Needs**

# BREAK OUT

**Do you ever look around you and just think that this journey we call 'life' is all a little bit crazy?**

And why everything is laid out for us as soon as we are born to follow a certain path? But does this path necessarily lead to fulfillment and happiness? Who are the architects of this path and what is their agenda?

Five years ago I asked the same questions to myself was I living or just existing? This led me on a journey of deep research and discovery both of the outer World around me, and my own inner World. I realised that a lack of understanding leads to a lack of fulfillment and purpose in life, so this book is an honest assessment of hard hitting questions about beliefs and traditions we as species have held for eons.

I found that many problems exist because these beliefs are never explored or probed with a critical eye, and indeed once re-evaluated can potentially lead to a much deeper understanding of where and how we fit into this mad World. Everything in this book is uncensored and from the heart, and from a place of wanting a better World for everyone both individually and collectively.

SAZMICK
BOOKS
WWW.SAZMICKBOOKS.COM     UK RRP: £13.33

www.ingramcontent.com/pod-product-compliance
Lightning Source LLC
Chambersburg PA
CBHW022110090426
42743CB00008B/795